THE
FORMOSA FRAUD

The story of the
FAKE WRITINGS
OF
GEORGE PSALMANAZAR
ONE OF THE GREATEST
CHARLATANS
IN
LITERARY HISTORY

With the full text of his book
"A DESCRIPTION OF FORMOSA"
And extra writings on his alleged travels
and his
SPURIOUS RESPONSES
TO
SKEPTICAL OBJECTIONS

Graham Earnshaw

The Formosa Fraud

By Graham Earnshaw

ISBN-13: 978-988-8422-12-8

This book has been reset in 10pt Book Antiqua. Spellings and punctuations are left as in the original edition.

HISTORY / Asia / Formosa

EB079

Published by Earnshaw Books Ltd. (Hong Kong)

Contents

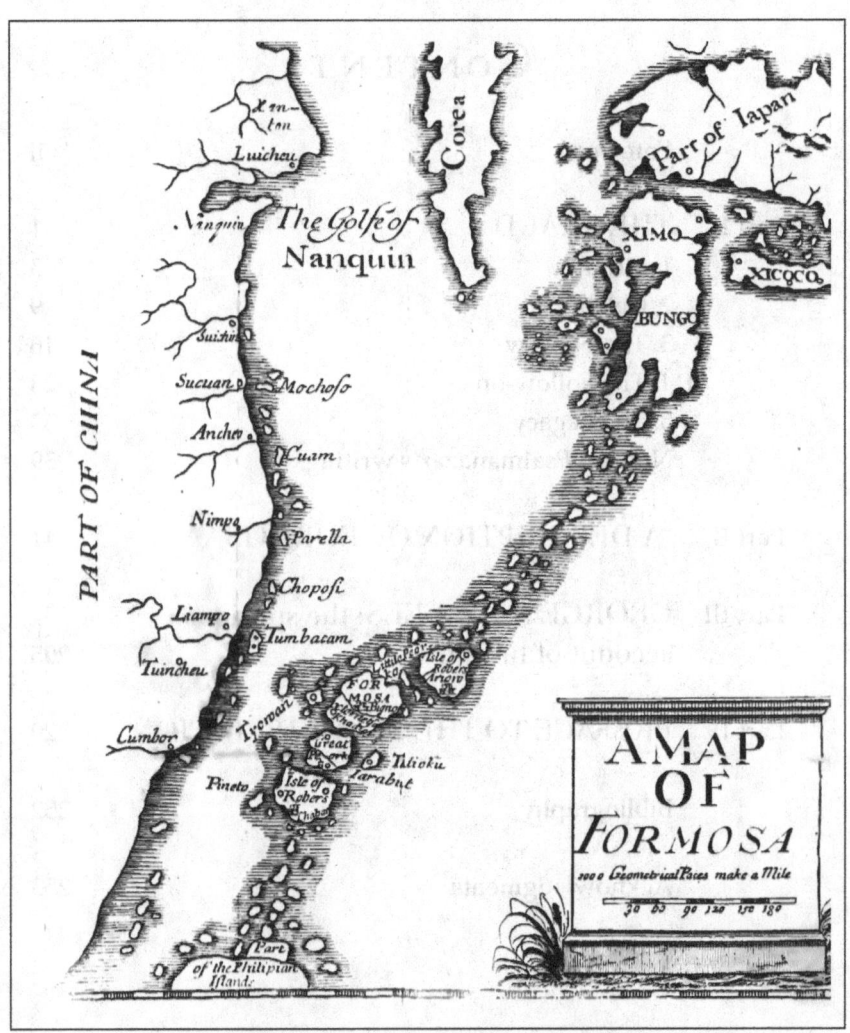

Psalmanazar's semi-fantasy map of Formosa and environs

FOREWORD

FAKERY IS A PART of life. Telling one hundred percent of the truth one hundred percent of the time is just not possible for anyone, nor advisable.

The truth about dishonesty is that most of it is modest in nature — simple lies of omission, slight obfuscations, the dressing up of inconvenient facts, putting a somewhat generous spin on unfortunate circumstances. There would be few CVs that have ever been sent out that are totally and completely honest in terms of the experience and qualifications and capabilities listed. Marketing and public relations are two huge professions that are wholly dedicated to putting lipstick on reality — and the astute consumer of products and information is, on one level or another, in on that "secret."

But fakery in information is taking on a new significance these days. Social media, which we have all come to depend on to some extent, is flooded with fake news, something that played an important, maybe even decisive, role in the 2016 U.S. Presidential election. The irresistible pull of marketing gravity sucks in the mainstream media as well, unwillingly or all-too-willingly. And then there are the accusations that the same media are themselves pushing "fake news."

As a former journalist and someone who deals every day with the shadowy dividing line between fact and spin, reality and hype, lies and the truth, the story of George Psalmanazar was particularly appealing because it is not simply a story of the past. It has a relevance to today, as we try to make sense of the flood of information coming at us unfiltered through our myriad devices, or worse, filtered by an algorithm optimized for click-throughs instead of the "public good."

The sense of general unreliability of information, of individuals being left to make up their own minds as to the veracity or fakeness of what they are told would have been as true for people in London in the early eighteenth century who heard the stories of Formosa told by George Psalmanazar as for viewers of various YouTube channels today. The difference is that today, we have the means, if we choose to use them, of verifying information in various ways. In 1704 in London, there was no Google, no fact-checking websites and no easy way for anyone to call Psalmanazar on any details of his story. And he used that fact, the inaccessibility of the source material, to his advantage. But in many cases today, the existence of evidence to the contrary hardly slows down the wildly implausible, to say nothing of the merely mistaken, just as the authorities of the days — Jesuit priests who had lived many years in China — were not necessarily believed when they called Psalmanazar out on details of his fantasy.

There are many parallels to situations and events in modern times, but the experience of James Frey seems particularly apposite. Frey is an American writer whose book "A Million Little Pieces" was published in 2003 as a memoir. It includes sometimes harrowing stories of his years growing up, and even Oprah Winfrey, who unlike the rest of us is surrounded by specialists who professionally manage her life, bought into it. Frey was eventually exposed, and admitted that many episodes in the book were either exaggerated or plain made up. But in an interview in 2006, Frey defended his work, saying that all memoirs change some details for literary effect. Oprah also took the view, in part, that regardless of the issues, Frey's story had been inspirational for her viewers... a claim that, one should note, is useful in its in-built resistance to verification.

There are perhaps two common themes that can be discerned in a comparison of the many examples of fake news today and the story of George Psalmanazar. One is a determination on the part of the faker to double down in the face of objections. Do not admit the lie, instead build on it. Be categorical. Cast doubt on the objector, and accuse them fakery too. The second theme is a desire on the part of the audience to believe the lie. Just like Oprah with Frey, English readers including the Bishop of London saw a fantastic story in Psalmanazar story something that was useful to them.

With Psalmanazar's tales of riches and exoticism in a corner of far-off Asia, there was a ready audience in the early eighteenth century ready and primed to lap it up, embracing the Formosa fantasy for their own reasons regardless of, even in the face of, obvious flaws to the story. The link between this story and how information flows and audiences deal with it in the early twenty-first century is obvious.

Many people have told a white lie to get their first job, to get on that crucial first rung of the ladder. There is an English saying that "First you get on, then you get honest." Which says much the same thing – fake it if need be until you are in a position to be real. Psalmanazar just took the same idea and built it out with a creativity that in some ways matches J.R.R. Tolkein's Middle Earth.

This is not in any way a defence of fakery or of Psalmanazar, but simply a recognition of the universality of the psychology involved. Social media in the early twenty-first century has provided an opportunity for doing exactly the kind of thing that Psalmanazar did – the creation of an entire castle in the air. The silo-ed and discrete nature of online social media communities recreates in a way the geographical distances and difficulties of travel that made it possible for Psalmanazar to pull the wool over the eyes of Londoners all those years ago.

Graham Earnshaw

PART I

THE
FRAUD

1. Origins

Taiwan is the topic on everyone's lips. What's going on there? Who does the island rightfully belong to? How important is the influence of the West? What is the real culture of the island's residents? The debate rages.

Is this the early twenty-first century? No, it's London more than three hundred years ago, at the beginning of the eighteenth century.

In 1704, a man appeared in England with the most extraordinary stories about Taiwan, or Formosa as it was then called. Eighteen-thousand boys are killed every year as part of Formosan religious ceremonies, the island is a major producer of gold and silver and Catholic priests are causing trouble there.

He said his name was George Psalmanazar, and his information about Formosa — it's culture, history, society and economy — absolutely captivated the English reading public. He published a book on the topic which went into a second edition, he gave speeches, he was fêted by the Bishop of London, he went to Oxford to teach Formosan. There was just one problem with the situation - his whole story was fake.

George Psalmanazar knew nothing of Formosa, had never been anywhere closer to it than Avignon in the south of France. And yet with enormous skill and creativity, he created an entire world around the idea of Formosa, including a fake language, a fake religion and a fake history.

The choice of Formosa for this story is somewhat serendipitous, but Formosa was then, and to an extent remains today, a place in exotic East Asia that is both separate and not separate, a place that is both known and also not fully understood. It is, most importantly, an island, and it was that fact that George Psalmanazar used as the basis of his web of deceit.

But to what purpose?

George Psalmanazar was born somewhere around the year 1679, and while the exact date is not known, it was certainly not with that name.

He became famous for pretending to be a Formosan, a fabrication which for a time made him a celebrity in London, but his *Memoirs*, published the year after his death in 1764, indicate that he was born in southern France, for he had long since given up the fiction that he was a native of that island off the coast of China which today is called Taiwan.

He says in the *Memoirs* that his parents were Roman Catholics, but gives no further information about them, not even their names. An advertisement to the first edition of his *Memoirs* quotes from a clergyman and long-time acquaintance of his, who said that:

"He was a Frenchman. His pronunciation had a spice of the Gascoin accent, and in that provincial dialect, he was so masterly, that none but those born in the country could equal, none though born there could excel him."

It further suggests that the Languedoc region of southern France was his place of birth.

But Psalmanazar makes few references in his *Memoirs* to his very early years, beyond the suggestion that his family was poor, that his father left when he was less than five years old to live in what is today southern Germany, and that he was considered as a child to be a gifted student.

His delight in keeping his origins a secret was part of a lifelong game which far outlasted the Formosan scam. Here is an excerpt from his *Memoirs* showing how hard he worked throughout his life at the artifice by masking his accent and jumbling together phrases and pronunciations to make it impossible for anyone to figure out his origins. He clearly relished ever minute of it.

"My idiom and pronunciation were so mixed and blended, and I may say designedly so, by the many languages I had learned, and nations I had been conversant with, that it was impossible for the most curious judge to discover in it any thing like an uniform likeness to any other European one they knew of."

"The truth was," he added, "I knew enough of all of them to blend my discourse more or less with any of them, as either to put people upon the wrong scent, whilst I kept every one from getting into the right one; for I can safely say that I never met with, nor heard of any one, that ever guessed right, or any thing near it, with respect to my native country."

At six, he attended a school run by two Franciscan monks and learned Latin from them, and then attended a Jesuit college, where he studied the "Humanities," rhetoric and philosophy. He speaks proudly in the *Memoirs* of his early facility for learning languages, not surprising for someone who would go on to create one (or to at least to fake it up to some reasonable level of depth and complexity in terms of grammar and vocabulary). After that he went to study philosophy and theology in a Dominican university in the same region of France, and was, he says, by far the youngest of the pupils, "some of whom were twice my age, and none by many years so young as I."

At sixteen, he moved on to Avignon where he says he continued his studies and started working as a tutor, teaching young gentlemen some of what he had learned of Latin, philosophy and theology. But he says that his attractive appearance caused him trouble. The mother of two boys he was tutoring made sexual advances to him, and dismissed him when he did not respond in the desired way.

"As she was a sprightly lady, and her spouse somewhat heavy, though not old, I soon found by her behaviour, and her parting beds with him soon after my coming, that she would have been better pleased I had transferred my care from them to her; and as I was naturally fond of ingratiating myself with the sex, I indulged her in all her little foibles, but without having the least design of going farther than a bare complaisance, in order to gain her esteem and admiration, rather than her affection."

His decision not to respond to her overtures, he said, was the result of "my natural sheepish bashfulness, and unexperienced youth" rather than virtue. After six months he was dismissed.

He returned to Avignon, down and out, and explained his ragged appearance to people by saying he was "a sufferer for religion for too great attachment to the church." A first tentative subterfuge.

He decided to return home, and that triggered his next, more elaborate, scam. To help convince people to give him money along the way, he stole a cloak and staff and forged a certificate stating that he was a "student in theology, of Irish extract" on a pilgrimage to Rome. He went first to see his mother and then set off north to see his father, who encouraged Psalmanazar to visit other parts of Germany and the Netherlands before he returned to France. By now, he had given up the Irish identity because it was too easy for people to call him on the ruse – there were people on the road who could tell the difference between a real and a fake Irishman. He therefore changed his story and chose for himself a new place of origin that virtually no one in Europe could question. He became Japanese.

He made himself a new certificate of identity, and invented an alphabet and various words of a language that he hoped would be mistaken for Japanese. He knew that Hebrew was written from right to left, so he deduced that other Eastern languages would follow suit. He came up with twenty letters with shapes and pronunciations that drew on Greek and Hebrew letters for inspiration.

To support his story, he also created, he says in the *Memoirs*, "many other particulars equally difficult, such as a considerable piece of a new language and grammar, a new division of the year into twenty months, a new religion, &c. and all out of my own head."

In fact it was ten months; his memory of the details of his own invention had faded over the years. Unwell and also destitute, he was dragooned into a military unit near Bonn, using his new Japanese persona, then shifted to another regiment in Cologne, when for the first time he used the name Psalmanazar. He says in his *Memoirs* that he took the name from the Bible; Shalmaneser was a king of Assyria who held the Israelites captive. He later changed the spelling, adding an initial P, he said, to make it more exotic.

He also further changed his story, saying he was in fact from the island of Formosa, now called Taiwan, which he said was politically and culturally subservient to Japan.

Now in his early twenties, Psalmanazar changed regiments again, this time enlisting in a unit at Sluys, Holland, where he met a Scottish chaplain named Alexander Innes who quickly saw through Psalmanazar's fraud.

"His stratagem," Psalmanazar wrote in his *Memoirs*, "was to make me translate a passage of Cicero *de natura deorum*[1] of some length, into my (pretended) Formosan language, and give it to him in writing; and this I easily did ... But, after he had made me construe it, and desired me to write another version of it on another paper, his proposal, and the manner of his exacting it, threw me into such visible confusion, having had so little time to excogitate the first, and less to commit it to memory, that there were not above one half of the words in the second that were in the first."

Innes told him, with a wink, that he "ought to take care to be better provided for the future."

Innes in other words, also saw an opportunity in the situation, and once he was sure that Psalmanazar had the wit to sustain the fraud, he wrote to the Bishop of London introducing this extraordinary pagan from a far-off land whom he had baptized into the Church of England. Psalmanazar, broke and tired of the military life, was happy to play along, and Innes obtained for him an invitation to go to England. Innes, for his part, received a personal commendation from the Bishop of London, Henry Compton.

They sailed for England. Psalmanazar wrote that he was so worried during the trip across the Channel about whether he could maintain the charade that he paid little attention to a fierce storm that threatened the ship to such an extent that many of the passengers, Innes among them, took to a long boat just in case the ship foundered.

But once they had landed at Harwich and Innes took him to celebrity London, the advantages of the scam started to become clear.

---

1   Cicero's *Nature of the Gods*

2. Celebrity

HE AND INNES moved into lodgings on Pall Mall and Innes started introducing him round. Psalmanazar, masquerading as a Formosa pagan newly escaped from the Jesuits and welcomed into the Church of England, became a celebrity. Innes, meanwhile, was engaging, Psalmanazar said, in "notorious and barefaced immoralities."

"The truth is, he had an almost insurmountable propensity to wine and women, and when fraught with the former, fell immoderately foul on the latter, whether maids or married."

Psalmanazar would by this time have got over his youthful bashfulness and perhaps, who knows, took advantage of the curiosity of the local ladies towards a "Formosan."

Innes introduced him to the Bishop of London, and Psalmanazar started circulating in London society. Meanwhile, he was writing his description of Formosa, building on the initial stories he had weaved on the road and embellished for Innes. He wrote it, he said in the Preface, mostly in Latin.

Within a year of his arrival in England, Psalmanazar was famous. In 1704, he completed his book *An Historical and Geographical Description of Formosa* and it was published in London. He dedicated the book to Bishop Compton, with whom he had shared early drafts of his "Formosan" materials, including a translation of the Lord's Prayer and the Ten Commandments into Psalmanazar's fake Formosan script, a table of the Formosan alphabet, and drawings of the clothing of the Formosans, which appeared in the book as published.

The first edition was an instant success, but also raised the eyebrows of detractors who had already raised a range of objections to Psalmanazar's story in various meetings.

The pinnacle of Psalmanazar's credibility was reached

when he appeared, prior to the publication of his book, before the Royal Society, an organization created in 1660 to promote scientific and cultural enquiries of all kinds, which at the time of Psalmanazar's brief celebrity was headed by Sir Isaac Newton.

He spoke to members of the society on the topic of Formosa on February 2, 1704, debating against a French Jesuit priest, Father Jean de Fontenay, who had lived in China for fourteen years, before returning to Europe in 1702. He at least had had contact with other Jesuit priests who had spent some time in Formosa.

Psalmanazar said in the preface to the first edition that he defeated Fontenay's argument that Formosa was a tributary of China rather than of Japan, and dismissed many of the Jesuit priest's other assertions on the simple basis that they came from a Jesuit. He added that this was the first of three debates or discussions he had with Fontenay.

Psalmanazar does refer in his preface to the island of "Tyowan," which is what he says Fortenay called Formosa. Psalmanazar neatly muddies the waters by saying that although Tyowan existed, it was another island "somewhat remote and distinct from ours, and is now a colony belonging to the beforemention'd Dutch."

In the Second Preface, prepared and published in 1705, Psalmanazar, also gives an account of a meeting with astronomer and mathematician Edmond Halley which is worth quoting in full:

"'Tis about a Year since I had the honour to meet Captain Halley with some other Gentlemen at a Tavern," Psalmanazar said. "They ask'd me the usual questions about my Country, and I returned satisfactory answers. At last, says the Captain, Doth not the Sun shine down the Chimnies in Formosa? I answer'd negatively; at which they were surprized, for most Geographers place our Island under the Tropic of Cancer; but I went on, telling them that granting Formosa was exactly under the Line, it was impossible the Sun should shine down the Chimnies, for they do not stand perpendicular, but the Smoak is carried through the Walls of the House by crooked pipes, and their ends are turn'd directly upwards, the better to convey it into the Air.

"Pray Sir (says the Captain) when you stand upright in the hottest weather how is your Shadow? I reply'd very short, insomuch that it can scarcely be discern'd.

"The last question was, How much twilight we have in Formosa? At first I did not understand his meaning, for I then knew very little English; but when he had explained himself, I reply'd that I never made any observations about it, for till I came into Europe, I never heard of a distinguish'd time from Day and Night.

"This is the whole of our Conference, tho' some People are pleas'd to invent a great deal more."

For Psalmanazar, given his weird take on reality, it must have been an extraordinarily triumphal moment, when a peasant boy from southern France could go toe-to-toe with one of the greatest brains of his age, even if it was on the basis of lies and obfuscation. Halley challenged him with chimneys and Psalmanazar shut him up with an embellishment of crooked pipes.

He begins the Second Preface, which is largely made up of refutations of the objections raised against his story, by saying that he had not originally wished to provide credibility to the accusers by referring to them at all. But it was the booksellers who insisted. But the overall sense is he relished the opportunity to double down on the scam.

"I am so secure in my Integrity, that the little Cavils of these disingenuous and inhospitable Men do not move me," he wrote. "However, the importunities of others have prevail'd, and I shall proceed to satisfie those scrupulous Gentlemen."

In his *Memoirs*, published many decades later, Psalmanazar says that though the naysayers, including Halley, "judged rightly of me in the main," they made two errors. The first was that they did not focus on his weakest point, which was the fake language he had created.

"I had been so negligent, notwithstanding Mr. Innes's caution of being prepared, against exigencies, with a language and a prudent readiness at reading and writing my new invented character, that had I been attacked on that side, I must have been infallibly foiled," he said.

To his relief, his critics focused on other issues.

The Second error he said, was that his critics, primarily Edmond Halley, the doctor Richard Mead and naturalist John Woodward, worked too hard at trying to prove the falsity of his story, thereby creating ammunition for his supporters, who appreciated particularly the religious side of Psalmanazar's story.

"As I had then several zealous patrons of great candor and integrity, who made it their business to search into the bottom of those reports, they found so much sophistry and disingenuity in them, that I cannot but observe here, that the too visible eagerness of these gentlemen to expose me, at any rate, for a cheat, served only to make the more serious and candid part think the better of me, and to look upon me as a kind of confessor, especially as the three gentlemen abovementioned, but more particularly the first, were known to be no great admirers of the Christian revelation, to which my patrons thought I had given so ample a testimony."

Despite the doubts and the controversy, Psalmanazar had many supporters and Bishop Compton arranged for him to spend some time at Christ College at Oxford so he could teach the Formosan language there and prepare a second edition of the book, "whilst my opposers and advocates were disputing here about the merit or demerit of the first."

He spent close to six months in Oxford, and used much of the time to work on his act as a Formosan. He also wrote a long Second Preface for the new edition of the book, which addressed in great detail many of the objections that had been raised.

He is almost apologetic in terms of how he had attained such a position of respect in the hallowed halls of Oxford under false pretenses:

"When I came to the university, I found many learned and worthy friends as warmly engaged for, as others were against me; and with this seeming advantage on my side, at which I have had frequent occasion to blush, that the former were men of the best character for candor and probity, as well as learning and parts, and whom, for that very reason, I forbear, as I ought, to name."

Psalmanazar's tutor at Oxford, possibly Samuel Reynolds, was apparently completely taken in by the Formosa scam and was very supportive.

He socialized most days and evenings, but usually retired to his apartment by nine o'clock, he said, to keep up the pretence that he was a real scholar:

"To make a shew, at least, of retrieving the time I wasted abroad in the day-time in company, music, &c. I used to light a candle, and let it burn the greatest part of the night in my study, to make my neighbours believe I was plying of my books; and sleeping in my easy chair, left the bed often for a whole week as I found it, to the great surprize of my bed-maker, who could hardly imagine how I could live with so little sleep."

People showed concern at his lack of sleep, and he responded with yet another charade.

"I began to pretend to have swelled legs and feet, and a gouty kind of distemper, which my friends failed not to attribute to that, and earnestly intreated me tosubmit to more regular hours and method of rest," he wrote. "My pretended lameness gave me a kind of gravity, which I was not willing to part with, not knowing how to keep up to the one without the other, I went still limping about like an old gouty fellow, though no man could enjoy a better share of health and flow of spirits than I did all the time I staid there."

As he largely idled away his time in Oxford, he completed an expansion and embellishment of the first edition, including new information about cannibalism, devil worship and the subjugation of Formosan women. He also wrote a second preface with answers to the objections, "which, all things considered, met with much greater approbation than it deserved, from those few intimates I had shewed it to."

Which suggests that even decades later, he was quite pleased with himself for the way he extended and deepened his web of lies to offset the actually perfectly reasonable objections raised.

On his return to London from Oxford, he went back to the same lodgings on Pall Mall to find that Innes had moved on.

"I was told that he was gone over chaplain-general to the English forces in Portugal. I had no reason to regret his absence."

The second edition of the book was simultaneously published by three printers in London, including one located in Fleet Street, at the price of six shillings. Psalmanazar says in posthumously published *Memoirs* that he received ten guineas for the first edition of the book and twelve guineas for the second edition, "besides such presents as were made me by the generous few to whom I presented them."

The second edition contains a lovely and obviously spurious "map" of Formosa in relation to Japan, China and the Philippines, as well as the long new preface, dated June 12, 1705, which includes the list of the twenty-five objections he chose to address, to each of which he gives answers.

It is interesting to ponder his state of mind as he wrote and published this, embellishing the original story, digging the hole of his forged past even deeper. Along with the glee of the extended fraud, there must have been fear at the possible consequences of exposure. He had some formidable intellectual artillery ranged against him, and the more detail he gave on his "Formosan" past, the more material was available for the naysayers to blow apart. On the other hand, what a thrill to fool England into thinking that he came not from southern France but from an island in the Exotic East! The mindset of an imposter is not an easy thing to fathom.

3. The Fantasy

HIS DESCRIPTIONS OF Formosa are often fantastic, but include touches of description that would have at least some familiarity for his English readers. It was a tough line to walk – too alien would have been unbelievable, while too ordinary would have been uninteresting. There is a long section, for instance, on the garb of the Formosan priests, the description of which is reminiscent of Catholic priest raiments in Europe.

His explanation of how he left Formosa and made his way to Europe had to stand up to some considerable cross-examination and the story he created, as given in a new section in the Second Edition entitled "Account of the Travels," revolved around a Jesuit priest – a figment of his imagination, of course – named Father de Rode, who he says had spent time in the Portuguese colony of Goa on the Indian coast, learning Japanese before traveling on to Formosa where he masqueraded as a tutor to escape the ban on Christian proselytizing in Japan and its territories (Psalamanazar's position, finally to become reality in 1896, was that Formosa was subject to the Japanese empire).

Psalmanazar's story was that La Rode was taken on by his father in Formosa to teach him Latin, as a result of which he says he gave up the study of Greek – a detail which should have been a massive red flag for anyone suspecting a fraud. But perhaps for many English readers in the early 18th century, Greek was as "Greek" as anything further eastwards.

Father de Rode was passing himself off in Formosa as Japanese, just as Psalmanazar would later pass himself off in England as a Formosan. And also as a Japanese gentleman who spoke fluent Latin. What a wonderful web he had spun.

So after four years as his Latin teacher, Father de Rode told Psalmanazar that he intended to leave Formosa, and go traveling around the world, and the nineteen-year-old boy, excited by de Rode's descriptions of strange and distant lands, insisted that he be allowed to come along too. Psalmanazar's fantasy alter-ego stole twenty-five pounds of gold from his father and set off with the priest on a boat that sailed south to the Philippines, where they found berths on a ship heading for Goa. From there, they sailed to Gibraltar and traveled on to France, where de Rode took him to a Jesuit monastery in Avignon, home territory for the real Psalmanazar.

There, the Jesuits tried by threat of force to convince him to convert to Catholicism, but the Psalmanazar alter-ego did not understand much of their arguments and so de Rode had to explain it to him in the Japanese language. Makes perfect sense.

The Jesuits gave him a deadline of fifteen days by which he had to convert, or else be handed over to the Inquisition, and on the tenth day, the Psalamanazar alter-ego made a run for it. He tried to leave the city wearing his "Japan" clothes and was stopped by the guard at the city gate. He then changed into local garb and tried again, also to be recognized and stopped. This time, he bribed the guard by giving him a pistol, and the guard let him go.

He traveled north, he said, to the town of Andernach in Germany where he was pressed into a local regiment, in spite of declaring himself to be a Pagan from Formosa. This part of the story presumably parallels Psalamanazar's true experiences quite closely, as he was already posing as a "Japanner" at that time in real life. His *Memoirs* do not mention Andernach, but do tell of traveling to Cologne, which would have taken him through Andernach and given him the information necessary to support that part of the story.

The flights of fancy that Psalmanazar engaged in as he built out his vision of the fantasy world of Formosa included, as fairly random examples, the assertion that elephants and camels are indigenous to the island and widely used for transport, the Japanese language has three genders, and the island is free of venereal disease, or as he calls it, French-pox, "because they allow Polygamy and prohibit Adultery." The priests of the Formosan religion, furthermore, speak Greek.

Some of his descriptions of Formosa are reminiscent of the Aztec world, especially in relation to the temples and religious ceremonies. There are references that echo descriptions of Japan in that era, and also some influence from a book by Bernhardus Varenius called *Descriptio regni Japoniae et Siam*, published in 1649. But Psalmanazar largely ignored a real description of Formosa by a Dutchman named Georgius Candidius, published in 1664, for reasons he explains in a cunning answer given below.

But most of the book is a pseudo-European fantasy straight out of the brain of Psalamanazar, an extended, detailed and phenomenal work of fiction.

What is a surprise is the incredible and preposterous detail into which Psalamanazar goes. Here is an example related to the alleged social formalities of greetings, which is breathtaking in its ludicrous detail:

"They Salute the Kings by bending their Knee, joyning their Hands and bowing their Head. They Salute the Vice-Roys also by bending one Knee, (viz. The Left, if he be the Vice-Roy of a Foreign King, and the Right if he be Vice-Roy of one of his own Kings) and also by carrying his Right Hand from his Head down to the ground. They Salute an High-Priest as they do a King, and the chief Sacrificators as they do ViceRoys. The Noblemen and Priests are Saluted by carrying the Hand from the Head down to the shoe, and by bowing the Head. One Friend Salutes another by kissing both his Hands, and joyning them with his Friends, Superiors do not Salute an Inferior, but by a nod of their Head they signify, that they have seen him Saluting them. Servants Salute their Masters, by carrying their Hand from their Mouth down to the ground, and falling prostrate on their Face. Wives do Salute, and arc Saluted after the same manner as their Husbands."

His delightful Formosan "calendar" casts it as having been decreed by the great prophet:

"Ye shall divide the Year into 10 Months, which ye shall call by the Names of the 10 Stars, viz. Dig, Damen, Analmen, Anioul, Dattibes, Daber, AnalJer, Nedzem, Koriam, Turbam. Every Month shall have four weeks, and five of these Months shall have 37 days, viz. the first, 3d. 5th. 7th. and 9th, the other 5 shall have only 36 days, Every week shall have 9 days, but in the Months which have 37 days, the last week shall have 10 days, and the 10th. shall be a day of Fasting."

And 37 times five plus 36 times five does actually equal 365, which is very mathematically neat of George. Disappointingly, he fails to address leap years.

His comment on the health situation in Formosa should have also raised some eyebrows.

"The greatest Disease to which the Natives are Subject is the Plague," Psalmanazar wrote, "which they believe does not proceed from Natural Causes, but from the common consent of the Sun Moon and Stars, who agree in sending it for a Punishment to Men, and therefore they rather make use of Sacrifices than

Medicins for the cure of it. This does not happen frequently, for 'tis now 170 years, since there was a Plague in Formosa ..."

In other words, the plague is the worst disease on the island, but there had not been an outbreak for 170 years, meaning that no one alive could have experienced it. He still gives a detailed explanation of how the Formosans deal with the sickness.

Another comment, possibly related to the circles into which he had been thrown after arriving in London, was that Formosans live longer than English people because they don't drink alcohol.

And this wonderful and surely tongue-in-cheek description of a Formosa disease:

"Maids, for the most part, when they come to be 18 or 20 years Old, are troubled with a certain Disease, which we call Chatarsko, and here in England, is called the Green-Sickness, which makes them Melancholy, and destroys all their appetite to any thing except Matrimony, corrupts the Blood, and makes them pale colour'd. This Disease is peculiar to the Female Sex, for which there is no other Remedy but Marriage."

He says at one point that the name of Psalmanaazaar, one of the two prophets who brought religion to the island, means "The Author of Peace." The religion of Formosa as constructed by George is beyond gobbledegook and while well worth reading about in the Description for entertainment value, but it is not worth analyzing beyond saying that it contains weird suggestions and echoes of some Catholic practices.

George provides a history of Formosa which is wondrous in the colorful complexity of its claptrap. One image that sticks in the mind is his description of a huge statue in one of the cities of Formosa of an elephant balanced on its hind legs spouting water from various orifices.

"This Fountain is believ'd by the Jappannese to have been built above 11500 Years ago, by a certain God or hero, who had been Banish'd thither when the Isle was yet uninhabited."

Then, in a typical mish-mash of historical whimsy, George also summarizes the history of Japan, in the context of explaining the Formosan language:

"The reason why the Japan Language differs from that of the Chinese and Formosans, is this, because the Japannese being banish'd from China, settled in the Isles of Japan; upon which account they so much hate the Chinese, that they have chang'd all things they had in common with them, as to their Language, Religion, &c. So that there is no affinity between the Japan and Chinese Language. But the Japannese being the first Inhabitants of Formosa, brought their Language along with them into that Island, which is now much more perfect than it was at their first coming."

He also provides a made-up history of the Jesuits in Japan which is so farcical and full of holes that one has to wonder what he was thinking as he was constructing it. The Jesuits, he said, managed to convert as many as a third of the Japanese citizenry including the Japanese emperor himself, and had worked out plans for the Spanish to seize all the main Japanese cities, before the anti-Christian mob descended on them and slaughtered them. The Japanese emperor, he further says, was forced into exile and died in Goa.

When the Japanese took over Formosa, some time after this according to Psalmanazar's fantasy timeline, they burned or crucified all the Jesuit priests they found there but were more lenient to Formosan Christian converts.

The point of the story for Psalmanazar, presumably, was to show what evil, duplicitous and untrustworthy the Jesuits were and how disastrous the consequences of their perfidy, queering the pitch for honest Christians of the right denomination looking to convert the locals in places like Japan and Formosa.

His *pièce de resistance* of creative fabrication was his section on the Formosan language.

"The Language of Formosa is the same with that of Japan, but with this difference that the Japannese do not pronounce some Letters gutturally as the Formosans do," is how he begins his description and then weaves a web of laughable linguistic lies that assumes that no one would be able to call him on not only Formosan but also the Japanese language. Even in the early 18th century, that was a bold step.

He then gives some examples of the Formosa language:

"That the Reader may have some Idea of the Formosan Language, I have here subjoin'd the Lord's Prayer, the Apostles Creed, and the ten Commandments in that Language, printed in Roman Characters.

The Lord's Prayer, called "Koriakia Vomera" in Psalmanazar's Formosan language, begins as follows:

Our Father who in Heaven art, Hallowed be thy Name ...
Amy Pornio dan chin Ornio viey, Gnayjorhe sai Lory,

Finally, he makes the astonishingly wild assertion that when the Japanese took over the Isle of Formosa, they so liked Psalmanazar's fake writing system that they adopted themselves, and largely abandoned use of the Chinese characters.

On and on he goes, truly a master of invention. But he pauses once in a while to implicitly consider the implausibility of it all.

"The history I do not deliver for a certain Truth," he slyly declares, "but neither do I account it altogether fabulous; for it seems to me very probable that there is something of truth in it."

He was similarly brazen in his response to those who believed he was making it all up, and in the Preface to the second edition, he included a wonderful riposte to the charges of forgery:

"He must be a Man of prodigious parts, who can invent the Description of a Country, contrive a Religion, frame Laws and Customs, make a Language, and Letters, &c, and these different from all other parts of the World, he must have also more than a humane Memory that is always ready to vindicate to many feign'd particulars, and that without ever so much as once contradicting himself."

Which is, of course, exactly what he did.

He forgave his critics, saying, "I do not imagine upon my return to Formosa, that even my own Countrymen will readily believe my Description of *England* and other parts of Europe." But he also expressed astonishment "that the censorious People here would have err'd so absurdly, as to take me rather for one of their Neighbours than for what I really am, a Japanese, born in Formosa, an Island many thousand Leagues distant from this of Great Britain."

One pertinent objection concerned Psalmanazar's spurious claim that Greek was used widely in Formosa, and his delightful answer is basically that if you don't believe me, go to Formosa yourself and see for yourself; prove me wrong if you can.

Another objection he addresses in the Second Preface was geographical – how did the Formosan mariners who supposedly took him and Father de Rode to the Philippines know their way there, given that Japan and Formosa forbad any contacts with the outside world?

Psalmanazar's answer is puzzlingly detailed in its fabrication, because it would have been easy for any sea captain or navigator with experience of the area to know it was false, whereas detail on language and social customs would have been much harder to question. He even included a fake map in the second edition to back up his contention that the sea between Formosa and the Philippines, like the sea between Formosa and Japan, is littered with small islands, making it impossible to get lost. (There are a few islands northeast of Taiwan and southwest of the main Japanese islands and a handful more between Taiwan and Luzon island in the south but nowhere near as many as represented on the Map.)

Psalmanazar was, quite rightly, queried on his obviously incongruous skin colour, which was European Caucasian fair. Why is your skin not darker, like other people from Asia? the naysayers asked. Ah, said Psalmanazar, the Formosan nobility basically live in holes:

"The Men of Estates, but especially the Women, are very fair; for they during the hot season, live under ground in places that are very cold; They have also Gardens and Groves in them so thick set with Trees, that the Sun cannot penetrate thro' them."

In his *Memoirs*, he expanded on this:

"My complexion, indeed, which was very fair, appeared an unanswerable objection against me; there being but few such to be met with in those hot climates, especially that of Formosa, which lies under the tropic; but by the help of what I had read or heard of some of those countries, I soon hatched a lucky distinction between those whose business exposes them to the heat of the sun, and those who keep altogether at home, in cool shades, or apartments under ground, and scarce ever feel the least degree of the reigning heat. And this distinction indeed is not only very reasonable, but was afterwards confirmed by persons of candor and experience, who had been in those countries, and affirmed that they had seen persons as fair as any northern Europeans, tho' not in so great a number, that lived under the rays of a vertical sun."

He clearly loved the possibility that his story might have been true more than he felt shame for the fact that it was a lie.

Psalmanazar was asked the name and nationality of the ship that allegedly took him and the good Father de Rode from Goa to Gibraltar, as well as the name of the captain, and his reply was that he didn't know. It was a crucial piece of information which would have given the lie to the whole story, so he had no choice but to be vague.

"I never expected to be called to an account for such trifles," he fumed in feigned outrage, "otherwise I would have noted down every thing I had seen and heard, for nothing less I find will satisfie these carping Cricticks. Could I imagine the Europeans would deny my Birth? Or could I think them so absur'd as to take me for one of their Countrymen rather than a Formosan?"

An outrageous thought, indeed.

Psalmanazar's response to Objection 14 in the Second Preface is classic. The objection is, how come your description of Formosa differs so much from what we know of Formosa from other writers? A good question, which Psalmanazar turns to his advantage. If I had been a fraud, he says, I would have been smart to base my description on the existing materials.

Those materials included the publication in Dutch in around 1664 of *A Short Account of the island of Formosa* by Georgius

Candidius, a missionary who lived in Formosa under the Dutch administration for more than a decade.

"If any European has a mind to banter the World, and set up for a Formosan or a Chinese," says Psalmanazar brazenly, "his best way certainly is to read Candidius and others, and frame his Tale so that he may not be contradicted by the Romantick Authors that have already written of these Countries. Candidius (as I have told you in the first Preface) and others, say, That we have no Governour, No Laws, &c. Why then should I assert we have, and contradict them almost in every thing they say? These Men assure you also that We are meer strangers to Letters; Why then should I be such a Fool to invent an Alphabet, and a Language, purposely to lessen my own Credit?"

Psalmanazar was also challenged, quite rightly, on his outrageous claim that Formosan religious customs required the sacrifice of 18,000 boys each year.

"We can believe that human Victims have (tho' very rarely) been sometimes offer'd," the objection stated, "but that 18000 Boys should be yearly sacrific'd is incredible, for this practice would in a short time depopulate the Island."

Here is the precise reference to a fabrication that he surely regretted once he was called on it.

"Ye shall begin the Year from this day, which is the first day of the Month Dig, and the first of the Festival of 10 days, and at this Festival ye shall Sacrifice to me every Year the hearts of 18000 young Boys, under the Age of 9 Years."

But he wasn't going to back down, and his riposts are slyly plausible, one being that it is the boys who are killed and not the child-bearing females:

"We allow Polygamy," he said, "and that supplies us with a numerous Issue. Suppose then eighty Males and eighty Females born in one street, and grant that Sixty of the Males are sacrificed,

26

there will yet be left twenty Males for eighty Females, and there is no doubt but these Women will have as many Children as any eighty Women in another Nation where Polygamy is not lawful."

Another answer to the same question cleverly turns the issue back to England, referencing the large migration of English males out to other parts of the world every year in that era.

"Do but consider how many Men, all fit for Marriage, go out of this Kingdom every Year, some to the East or West-Indies, some to Portugal, Italy, Germany, Flanders &c. and then tell me if more of your Men are not yearly destroyed than we sacrifice Children. And sure then one would think that Formosa is not in so great danger of being depopulated as England, where it is now a common observation, that there are four times more Women than Men."

4. The Follow-on

NOTES IN THE JOURNAL of the Royal Society indicate that its fellows were convinced of the fraud by mid-1705, based on information received from various sources. Fellows like Halley and Woodward must have been chuckling from the beginning. But the society did not make any statement about Psalmanazar, possibly because it was likely that criticism from the Royal Society's "free-thinkers" would have encouraged those interested in helping the former pagan Psalmanazar to portray himself as a defender of revelatory religion.

But with the doubts and questions lined up against him, Psalmanazar gradually faded from being society's darling to being an almost invisible hack writer.

In his *Memoirs*, apparently written over many years and published the year after his death, he describes *the Description of Formosa* as "A mere forgery of my own devising, a scandalous imposition on the public," and in another place, "That vile and romantic account."

But it also appears that he was in many ways pleased with, and proud of, his invention. In his *Memoirs*, he warns people away from such artifice, saying they placed him in circumstances "more dangerous no man could hardly be in." He also says, however, that he lived by the following principle, throughout his life:

"There was one maxim which I could never be prevailed upon to depart from, viz. that whatever I had once affirmed in conversation, tho' to ever so few people, and tho' ever so improbable, or even absurd, should never be amended or contradicted."

In other words, once he had constructed his castle of lies in the air, he would only add to it, never dismantle any part of it. A proud gambler, he was sure he could always find a way, an explanation that would be plausible to counter any objection.

One wonders, when he started the performance under Innes' direction in London, how long he thought he could get away with the story. To be sure, Formosa was on the other side of the world, and a blank page to almost everyone in England, but the Dutch were already there, and he surely knew that at some point he would have to admit the fraud. What, then, was his end-game? He was probably running on the moment, egged on by Innes, whose own end-game was to disappear to Portugal.

His follow-on actually included a declared deep devotion to religion, which many people including Samuel Johnson, believed to be sincere.

In 1706 and in 1707, Psalmanazar published defences of himself that emphasized his allegiance to "revealed religion," and in 1710, he published two pamphlets defending himself against the rising chorus of skepticism on his claims. But the ruse was sure to fail eventually. In its March 16, 1711 edition, *The Spectator* made a joke about it by publishing a fake advertisement for April Fool's Day, proclaiming that:

> On the first of April will be performed at the playhouse in the Hay-market an Opera call'd The Cruelty of Atreus. N.B. The scene wherein Thyestes eats his own children, is to be performed by the famous Mr. Psalmanazar, lately arrived from Formosa: The whole Supper being set to Kettle-drums.

He made one last use of his supposed Formosa background before giving up the charade. He worked with a man named Pattenden to promote a kind of lacquer called "white Formosan work" but the project failed. He then passed through a number of roles, including tutoring, working as a clerk, painting ladies' fans and doing translations.

The translation work, presumably mostly French and Latin into English, provided a new direction, and he ended up becoming a writer with a steady flow of work in the gutter-end of London's journalistic and bookish world, known as "Grub Street."

He was, in short, a hack writer, and noted for his copious output more than the quality of his work. He provided contributions to some of the many compendia and encyclopedias published in that era. He wrote large sections of Samuel Palmer's *The General History of Printing* (1732), Emanuel Bowen's *A Complete System of Geography* (1744), and *An Universal History from the Earliest Account of Time* (1736-68). To this huge work, which in its second edition ran to twenty volumes, Psalmanazar contributed articles on many subjects, including a history of the Jews, ancient Greece and the Gauls.

Somewhere over these years, Psalamanzar became extremely devout in his religious beliefs, or at least he convinced others that he had. He said that the reading of William Law's book, *A Serious Call to a Devout and Holy Life*, published in 1728, had a big impact on him, and the young Samuel Johnson once said much the same thing. Johnson, as related by Boswell, later frequently praised Psalmanazar for his religious devotion.

Sir John Hawkins, in his book *Johnsonian Miscellanies* relates that Johnson "was very well acquainted with Psalmanaazar, the pretended Formosan, and said, he had never seen the close of the life of any one that he wished so much his own to resemble, as that of him, for its purity and devotion."

Asked whether he ever contradicted Psalmanaazar, Johnson said: "I should as soon have thought of contradicting a bishop."

When Johnson was asked whether he had ever mentioned Formosa to Psalmanazar, "he said he was afraid to mention even China."

In fact, there are several references in Boswell's Life of Johnson to Psalmanazar, and added together they suggest strongly that George was a constant drinking companion of the great man. He refers to a certain gentleman as being "of a club in Old-street, with me and George Psalmanazar."

At one point, Boswell asks Johnson about which acquaintances he consorted with most.

BOSWELL. 'Lord Orrery, I suppose.'

JOHNSON. 'No, Sir; I never went to him but when he sent for me.'

BOSWELL. 'Richardson?'

JOHNSON. 'Yes, Sir. But I sought after George Psalmanazar the most. I used to go and sit with him at an alehouse in the city.'

What a telling mark of a successful life, to be treated with such respect by Samuel Johnson!

But George could be a prickly companion, it would seem. During one conversation with a group of people including Johnson and Psalmanazar, presumably in a noisy alehouse hopefully just off Fleet Street, "one of the company provoked him (Psalmanazar) greatly by doing what he could least of all bear, which was quoting something of his own writing, against what he then maintained."

One might guess that the reference was to something related to Formosa.

Psalmanazar became a leading exponent of "revealed religion," the idea of visions, revelations, miracles and other means by which human beings could directly communicate with God, and be aware of God's existence through personal experience. In the 18th century, with rationalism and skepticism on the rise in English intellectual circles, this idea was increasingly under attack. David Hume was one of the leaders of this new approach. In 1753 Psalmanazar published anonymously a book entitled *Essays on the Following Subjects*, which offered a defence of revealed religion.

In 1762, Psalmanazar wrote to a friend, Thomas Birch, of his failing health and also made out his will in which he named as his executor and residuary legatee Sarah Rewalling, "my pious and worthy friend ... of this parish of St. Luke, in Middlesex."

The lady was also named as the publisher of the posthumous *Memoirs*, but nothing further is known of her or of her relationship with Psalmanazar.

It is possible that opium addiction was the primary cause of his demise. He refers in the preface to his *Memoirs* to "that vast quantity of laudanum I have been known to take for above these forty years." He warns others of the danger of the drug, but also partly attributes his own longevity to it.

He died aged eighty-four in London on May 3 of the following year, 1763, at Ironmonger Row, in the Parish of St Luke in today's Islington. His will, which was published as part of his *Memoirs*, gave directions for a humble burial "without any kind of coffin ... but only a shell of lowest value, and without lid or other covering which may hinder the natural earth from covering it all around."

Gentleman's Magazine said in its obituary that Psalmanazar was "known for many ingenious performances in different parts of literature."

5. The Legacy

PSALMANAZAR WAS in fact one of a number of literary forgers during that age when publishing was booming, and the known world was expanding, but information was scarce and contradictory. Others included the Scottish academic William Lauder, famous for mangling Milton, Thomas Chatterton who forged huge quantities of the writings of an imaginary 15th century monk, and James MacPherson, who "discovered" an epic poem from the mists of Gaelic history, published to huge acclaim as *The Works of Ossian* around the time of Psalamanazar's death.

Psalmanazar was one of the earliest of these frauds, and by far the most daring of them, in that he not only faked literary works, he faked himself, too. And, for a time, very successfully.

Psalmanazar's fraud is also relevant in the context of other China and travel sleights-of-hand. The list begins with Marco Polo, who may have travelled across Asia and spent all those years in the empire of the Great Khan, and then again, maybe not. There are experts who are highly skeptical of his claims in the *Travels* published around 1300 and think he might have instead spent a couple of decades on the shores of the Black Sea collecting travellers' tales from people arriving from the East along the Silk Road.

Then there is the possibly fictitious character John Mandeville, whose book *The Travels of Sir John Mandeville* first appeared some time after 1357, telling of alleged journeys in the 1320s through to the 1350s in the middle and near East, North Africa and as far as India. But who actually wrote it and how much of it was based on tales received rather than personal experiences is not known.

Nearer to our time, there is Edmund Backhouse, whom I include on the list with some reluctance. Backhouse was an Englishman and in the eyes of many a brilliant linguist and

33

Oriental scholar who lived in Peking from 1899 through to his death in 1944 and co-wrote books in the early 20th century with materials from the Manchu Imperial Court that some say were forged. I had the pleasure of publishing his China memoirs, *Decadence Mandchoue*, which details his activities in the Imperial Palace and his personal relationship with the old Empress Dowager. The editor Derek Sandhaus took the view, with which I concur, that while Backhouse's descriptions of court life and the doings of the Empress Dowager, "might not represent a true, unembroidered account of the facts… readers would be unwise to dismiss them out of hand for their outrageousness."

"Even if it were completely fabricated, and I do not personally believe it was, it would still be an engaging and often hilarious historical fiction by a well-informed linguistic genius," he added.

Which is not far from an assessment that could also be made of George Psalmanazar.

In Psalamanazar's case, the enthusiastic reception to his book reflected the growing thirst in Europe for knowledge about far-flung corners of the world, and also the paucity of accurate information available. It is also true that such frauds often include and even require a willingness on the part of the audience to believe, and the reading public in England were clearly ready for the stories of a Pagan alien about the mysteries of an almost-completely unknown part of Asia.

In the introduction to the book, he heaped praise on Bishop Compton, as well as vitriol on the Jesuits, all of which would have helped sales coming from such an apparently exotic personage. His embrace of revelatory religion ensured him a significant number of supporters to counter the intellectual skeptics.

Unusually, Psalamanazar outlived his exposure by many

decades, although it is not clear whether he ever publicly came clean or renounced his fraud prior to his posthumously published memoirs. But he lived to create another career for himself as an apparently devout Christian with revelatory leanings and a journeyman writer. The *Memoirs* particularly indicate his considerable facility with words: he writes well, although in the style of the day, he was a victim of verbosity.

The spell of Psalmanazar's faked story left a mark on the English psyche, indelible enough that Jonathan Swift, in his satire *A Modest Proposal*, published in 1729 while Psalmanazar was still alive, could refer to Psalmanazar in relation to his ironic suggestion that the Irish, to solve the problem of their poverty, should sell their children to the rich of England as food:

But in order to justify my friend, he confessed, that this expedient was put into his head by the famous Salmanaazor, a native of the island Formosa, who came from thence to London, above twenty years ago, and in conversation told my friend, that in his country, when any young person happened to be put to death, the executioner sold the carcass to persons of quality, as a prime dainty; and that, in his time, the body of a plump girl of fifteen, who was crucified for an attempt to poison the Emperor, was sold to his imperial majesty's prime minister of state, and other great mandarins of the court in joints from the gibbet, at four hundred crowns. Neither indeed can I deny, that if the same use were made of several plump young girls in this town, who without one single groat to their fortunes, cannot stir abroad without a chair, and appear at a play-house and assemblies in foreign fineries which they never will pay for; the kingdom would not be the worse.

In the end, how to view Psalmanazar? I would say he should be seen primarily as a forger proud of his creation, regardless of his posthumous recantations.

Even his *Memoirs* do not reveal his identity, which ultimately indicates that he defined himself more by the artifice of his fraudulence than by the true roots of his real self. The *Memoirs* were published with the following title page, even, replacing his real name, whatever it was, with a series of asterisks:

MEMOIRS of * * * *
Commonly known by the Name of
GEORGE PSALMANAZAR;
A
Reputed Native of FORMOSA.
Written by himself
In order to be published after his Death.
CONTAINING
An Account of his Education, Travels, Adventures, Connections,
Literary Productions, and pretended Conversion from
Heathenism to Christianity; which last proved
the Occasion of his being brought over into
this Kingdom, and passing for a Proselyte,
and a Member of the Church of England.

His choice of Formosa as the basis for his extended charade was random and ultimately irrelevant. But thanks to his artifice, he did manage to create a new world for himself, and transitioned through his web of ingenious and preposterous lies to a new existence as a religious activist and literary hack in the world's greatest city of the age, a persona that kept him occupied and probably more prosperous and in more interesting company than would have been the case in Gascony, or wherever it was that he was born.

He created and disseminated a fantasy that resonated with the English public, to the extent that even twenty years later, Jonathan Swift still felt it was relevant to make a reference to him.

He represented, fraudulently, an argument against Roman Catholicism and for the relatively new Christianity of personal revelation that cheered and encouraged a generation of nonconformists.

And, even if fraudulently, he inspired visions in the minds of his readers of an Exotic East which would in various indirect ways no doubt bear fruit in terms of the adventures of many Englishmen and women around the globe over the following two centuries of exploration and expansion.

Ultimately – and this is just a personal view – he has to be admired for his audacity.

THE FRAUD

NOTE

THE SECTIONS BELOW consists of the first edition of Psalmanazar's Description, along with two additions from the second edition – the Second Preface and the Account of the Travels, which is characterized in that edition as "Book Two."

The text has been kept as close as possible to the original, but the punctuation has in some cases been altered slightly, with some semi-colons and colons being changed to commas and periods.

G.A.E.

PART II

AN
HISTORICAL and GEOGRAPHICAL
DESCRIPTION
OF
FORMOSA,
AN
Island subject to the Emperor of JAPAN.
GIVING

An Account of the Religion, Customs,
Manners, &c. of the Inhabitants. Together
with a Relation of what happen'd to the Author in his Travels; particularly his Conferences with the *Jesuits*, and others, in several
Parts of *Europe*. Also the History and Reasons of his Conversion to Christianity, with his
Objections against it (in defence of Paganism)
and their Answers.

To which is prefix'd,
A PREFACE in Vindication of himself from
the Reflections of a *Jesuit* lately come from *China*,
with an Account of what passed between them.

By GEORGE PSALMANAAZAAR,
a Native of the said Island, now in *London*.

Illustrated with several Cuts.

LONDON:
Printed for *Dan. Brown*, at the *Black Swan* without *Temple-
Bar*; *G. Strahan*, and *W. Davis*, in *Cornhill*; *Fran. Cog-
gan*, in the *Inner-Temple-Lane*; and *Bernard Lintott*, at the
Middle-Temple-Gate in *Fleet-Street*. 1704.

41

PART II

AN
HISTORICAL *and* GEOGRAPHICAL
DESCRIPTION
OF
FORMOSA,
AN
Island subject to the Emperor of JAPAN
GIVING

An Account of the Religion, Customs, Manners, &c. of the Inhabitants. Together with a Relation of what happen'd to the Author in his Travels; particularly his Conferences with the *Jesuits,* and others, in several Parts of *Europe.* Also the History and Reasons of his Conversion to Christianity, with his Objections against it (in defence of Paganism) and their Answers.
To which is prefix'd
A PREFACE in Vindication of himself from the Reflections of a *Jesuit* lately come from *China,* with an Account of what passed between them.
By GEORGE PSALMANAAZAAR.
a Native of the said Island, now in *London.*
Illustrated with 16 pp. Photogravures.

CONTENTS

To the
Right Honourable
and

Right Reverend Father in GOD,

HENRY,

by Divine Providence,

Lord Bishop of *LONDON*,

AND ONE OF

Her MAJESTY's most Honourable

Privy Council

Iknow not, My Lord, whether what I now most humbly dedicate to Your Lordship, may merit your perusal, especially at this time, when your Lordship is busied about Affairs of the greatest moment. But since Your Noble Soul (be it concern'd about Things never so weighty and intricate) must be allow'd some Minutes to unbend, I submissively beg You could please to bestow some of them upon this Treatise; well-knowing, if your Lordship smile upon it, the World cannot dislike it.

The Europeans have such obscure and various Notions of Japan, and especially of our island of Formosa, that They can believe nothing for truth that has been said of it. But the prevailing Reason for this my Undertaking was, because the Jesuits, I found, had impos'd so many Stories, and such gross Fallacies upon the Publick, that they might the better excuse themselves from those base Actions, which deservedly brought upon them that fierce Persecution in Japan. I thought therefore it would not be unacceptable if I publish a short Description of the Island of Formosa, and told the Reasons why this wicked Society, and at last all that profess'd Christianity, were, with them, expell'd that Country.

My Lord,

I look upon my self as much obliged to Your Lordship, as ever Man was to his Patron, having experienc'd your Goodness ever since I came into England; I have therefore earnestly desir'd by any honest and humble way, to express my Gratitude; but tho' Your transcendent Generosity, and the meanness of my Fortune and Capacity, render it impossible for me to pay Your Lordship all that Respect, and Acknowledgment which are due for Your Lordship's many and great favours; yet since my present leisure and enjoyments are owing to Your Munificence, I most willingly lay hold on this Occasion, and consecrate the First-fruits of such Blessings to the Hand that bestow'd them upon me, now in the least doubting but Your Lordship, according to your wanted Charity and Goodness, will vouchsafed to receive this little Book as a thankful testimony how vastly I am indebted to You; and as such it is, with all Humility and Veneration offer' by,

My LORD,
Your Lordship's
Most Grateful and
Obsequious Servant,

George Psalmanazar

The Preface

WHEN I FIRST arriv'd in England, every one was curious to discourse
me about my own Country; and forasmuch as my account of
it was entirely new, they thought it my duty to publish it, and I
readily comply'd with their advice, both for my own ease and their
satisfaction. But when I had met with so many Romantick Stories
of all those remote Eastern Countries, especially of my own, which
had been impos'd upon you as undoubted Truths, and universally
believ'd, then I was much discourag'd from proceeding in my
Description of it; yet since Truth ought to dispel these Clouds of
fabulous Reports, and I could not escape uncensur'd even by my self,
should I (by my silence) suffer you to remain in ignorance, or rather
deceiv'd by misrepresentations, I thought my self indispensably
oblig'd to give you a more faithful History of the Isle of Formosa,
than as yet you have met with.

But before I enter upon this Subject, 'tis convenient I should
premise some few things. Since then (as I before observed) there
are such various Accounts, and all different from what I shall give
you, this is no Reason for me to elope the greater Credit, but I leave
it to the unbias'd Judge to prefer which he pleaseth, for 'tis not
so much my Concern to be reputed sincere, as 'tis really to be so.
But here I must entreat you diligently to observe what followeth,
because the Reputation of my Book depends much upon it. In the
first place there are several things in their Story which you are
oblig'd to suspect, because they contradict one another in those
Matters which every Relater assures you he has been an Eye-witness

of, since then their Tale is so inconsistent, there is very little in it
that you ought to depend upon. But that I may expose some of
their Falsehoods, I will stream then what I assert by the Authority
of some English Merchants trading to China, whose Relations are
much the same with mine, but vastly different from theirs. As for
example: Candidius, and others, in their Account of Formosa, tell
us, there is neither Monarchical nor Democratical Government
in the Island, that there is no Law nor Punishment against Theft,
Adultery, or Murther, and such Black Crimes, but every Man judgeth
and revengeth in his own Cade. For instance, if a Man rob me of a
hundred Pound, I may steal from him as much by way of reprisal. Is a
Man murthers me, any of my Family, or Friends, may, by the Murther
of him revenge mine; and so of Adultery, &c. They tell us farther, that
there is no Oeconomy or Order amongst the Natives, that they are
even Strangers to the distinction of Master and Servant, that neither
Mines of Gold or Silver are to be found there, and that they have no
Spices. In answer to which, let me tell you, that those Merchants I
before mention'd, inform us, that there is a Governour to whom they
paid large Customs for every thing they exported. If then there is a
Governour, certainly there must be Laws, let Candidius, and others,
say what they please. That they have Gold, Silver, and Spices also, is
likewise prov'd by those Traders, who have exported vast Sums of the
one, and large Quantities of the other.

Reason it self is sufficient to confute what they say of Anarchy
in our Island. For how is it possible for any Kingdom to stand, if no
Law or Degrees of Dignity are observ'd? or how can a Community be
preserv'd, if there are no Penal Statutes to correct Offenders? In my
Opinion, if every one was left to revenge himself, such a Place must
be a continued Scene of Murther and Rapine; especially since the
Formosans (as Candidius, and others would have you believe) do not
look upon these Facts as monstrous Crimes, but only as little Tricks
and Piccadillo's.

There are some likewise that tell you, that the Island of Formosa belongs to the Chann of China; but if so, why do the Chinese pay so great Tribute to our Governour? For the truth of this, I dare appeal even to the Dutch themselves, who are competent Judges in the Case, ever since the Emperor of Japan has given them leave to renew their Trade in Formosa, after they had many Years been banish'd from thence; as you may see in the Book, Chap. 37. Of the Success of the Dutch in Japan.[1]

1. I could here also add much more, which for brevity-sake I omit: For 'tis convincing enough to say, that he who so grosly errs in one particular, may reasonably be thought an unfaithful Relater of every thing else. But whether these ridiculous Story-Tellers above-mention'd, vend their Legends out of a Design, or for want of a true Knowledge of Matter of Fact, is not my Business now to enquire.

2. The second thing I would have you take notice of, is, That I pretend not to give you a perfect and complete History of my Island, because I was a meer Youth when I left it, but nineteen Years of Age, and therefore uncapable of giving an exact Account of it: Besides I have now been six Years from home, so many things of moment may perhaps slip my Memory which would have adorn'd the Description of my Country. But whatsoever I can recollect, I have freely publish'd; and I assure you, I have not positively asserted any thing which is not as positively true; but if I have said what I did not know, as a certain Truth, as such I have admonish'd you of it. I have discharged my Conscience, receive it as you please; for since I have done my Duty, I shall no more be concern'd about it.

---

1   The Dutch ruled significant parts of southern Taiwan as a colony from 1624 to 1662, and there was no question of the Japanese emperor providing approval for the Dutch presence there. The Dutch were forced out by Koxinga, a half-Japanese pirate. The Spanish also had a settlement in northern Taiwan for a time and the Kingdom of Middag, a collection of aboriginal villages based around today's Taichung on the west coast, survived right through the European colonial period and the Koxinga rule, to be finally subjugated by the Manchus who extended their invasion of China in the 1660s to Taiwan and finally took full control of the island in 1732.

3. In my Book I have told you the Reasons that mov'd my Country-
men to make so great a Slaughter of the Christians; for the Jesuits
then made such weak Excuses for themselves, that many, not without
Reason, believ'd they had other Designs than what they pretended;
I thought it therefore proper to give you from the Records and
Tradition of my Country, the best Account of these Matters I could.
In vain the Jesuits assign the Envy of our Pagan Priests, and the
Emulation of the Dutch, as the Causes of this Persecution, such
things could never induce us to treat so cruelly all that profess'd
Christianity: Certainly there was a Snake in the Grass, which they
would not, but I have discover'd. I am confident by my revealing this
and much more, I shall draw all the Spite and Malice of the Jesuits
upon me, of which I have already met with a notorious Instance in
Father Fountenay, who is lately return'd from China, having been
eighteen Years a Missionary there; this Man is now in London, and
some Body had told him I was publishing a Book, in which I speak
much against the Roman Church, and especially against the Jesuits:
This has so enrag'd him, that he endeavours by all means imaginable
to destroy my Credit, as I am daily inform'd by many Gentlemen;
to whom I only reply'd, Let him alone, I am little concern'd at what
such a suspicious Person says against me: The truth is, and will be,
I hope, evident, notwithstanding his Attempts to stifle it, so I shall
apply the Words of the Poet to him,

Parturiunt montes, nascetur ridiculus mus.[2]

I have had three Conferences with him, without coming to any
conclusion; the first was before the Royal Society, on Wednesday the
second of this instant February, when there was a Publick Meeting of
the illustrious Members of that celebrated Body: That he might the

---

2   "The mountains are in labor, a ridiculous mouse will be born". A quote from Horace, a
     reference to works that promise much at the outset but yield little in the end)

more easily defend himself, he had Notice of my coming. After we had saluted each other, we began our Discourse. The first Question that was propos'd to him, was, To whom doth the Island of Formosa belong? He presently reply'd, It was tributary to the Emperor of China. Some of the Gentlemen ask'd him how he knew it to be so; he quickly answer'd, That a certain English Ship call'd the Harwich, was by stormy Weather forc'd upon the Shore of Formosa; that five Jesuits were Passengers in it, one of them was drown'd, the other four escap'd to the Island, from whence they sent Letters to this Father Fontenay, who then was in a certain City in China. Father Fontenay writes to the Chann, or Emperor; the Chann sends a Letter to the Formosans, demanding them and the Ship; and so the Formosans were compell'd to restore both them and the Ship. I answer'd, That this Story was nothing to the purpose; for since we are not at Wars with the Chinese, if any of their Ships should be driven on our Coast, and the Chann should reclaim them, altho' we live not in his Dominions, we are in Justice oblig'd to restore them: And thus I then answered his Story. But it appears since by the Testimony of several Merchants, that the afore-mentioned Ship was cast upon the Coast of China, and not of Formosa: Had I known as much then, I would before the illustrious Society have detected the Falshood of the Jesuit; but mistrusting he might be mistaken in the Name of the the Place, and take another Island for Formosa, I desir'd him to tell me by what Name the Chinese call'd Formosa; he answer'd, That he knew no other Name for it but Formosa, or Tyowan; but it's very plain, not only from what I (who should know best) assert, but also from a certain Gentleman who has been in Tyowan, that it is an Island somewhat remote and distinct from ours, and is now a Colony belonging to the beforemention'd Dutch. This indeed he confess'd he was ignorant of. I told him farther, That the Chinese call our Island by the Name of Pak-Ando, which agrees with Gad-Avia, as we call it, both which signifie the Island Formosa. Pak, Pak, says he, there is not such a word in the whole Chinese Language, that ended with a Consonant as Pak doth; which is very false, for the Name of almost all their great Cities end with a Consonant, as Nanking, Kanton, Peking, &c.[3] When at my desire he discours'd in the Chinese Language, near half his Words terminated with Consonants: This was so plain a Contradiction, that all the Auditory observ'd it. At the same Meeting also he deny'd there was any variety of Languages, or Dialects, thro' the whole Empire of China, but that all the Natives spoke with one and the same Tongue; which when it was demonstrated to be false by many then present, he made no manner of Reply, only unreasonably and obstinately persisted in affirming what he before had said. At length, that if possible I might make the matter yet more plain, I told him, Either what all the Jesuits, and others, had written of the Chinese Language, was not true, or what he said must be false; for they assure us, the Chinese in every Province speak various Dialects,[4] and they have different Languages, according to their Degrees or Quality; as for instance, the Noble-men speak the Mandarin Language; the Bonzees, or Priests, use another for the Divine Service, which is unintelligible to the Lay-People; and the Plebeans a third; so that I told him, either they, or he, (pardon the expression) must lye grosly. But he endeavour'd by impertinent Shifts to excuse himself. He deny'd also, that the Chinese had any Tone in their Speech by which they distinguish the signification of a word. This I likewise affirm'd to be false: For I have, in Formosa, heard many Chinese talking together, but they seem'd to me rather to sing than discourse; besides, this contradicts what the Jesuits themselves tell us. At length, after so many Interruptions, we ended our Conference: Let the Reader judge who had the better.

---

3   In fact, Cantonese and some other southern Chinese languages or dialects include a "k" sounding glottal stop. So by pure coincidence, in this particular case, Psalmanazar was right and Fontenay wrong - assuming Fontenay actually advanced the argument that Psalmanazar says he did.
4   *Vide* The Lord's Prayer in a hundred languages.

I have since had two Assignations to meet him, once at my Lady Powis's,[5] another time at Sion-College; but he fail'd to answer the Appointments.

Eight Days after, being Wednesday the Ninth of February, I was to Dine with Dr. Sloane, Secretary to the Royal Society; where were present the Right Honourable my Lord Pembroke; his Excellency, Spanhemins, the King of Prussia's Envoy; another Noble-man, and this Father Fontenay; when he was ask'd by his Excellency, to whom the Island Formosa belong'd; he reply'd, Here is a young Man, (pointing to me) who is a Native of that Country, he can better inform you than I, who have only been in China. I then answer'd him, that it did belong to the Emperor of Japan. We had nothing else remarkable in this Conference; neither had he the Assurance at this time to say any thing more to me: He wondred indeed to see me eat raw Flesh; because, says he, the Chinese dress their Meat after the same manner as the Europeans, tho' at the same time he confess'd the Tartars differ'd from them in their Cookery; for they only warm'd their Flesh before they eat it.

A third time I met him in the Temple-Coffee-House in Devereux-Court in the Strand, near Temple-Bar, where several Noble-men were present; and there he ask'd me the Manner, Time, and Reasons of my leaving my Country; and I rightly informed him: Neither had he the Face to raise any Objections, unless that he never knew Father de Rhode, who brought me out of my Country.

I am well inform'd he takes a great deal of freedom in aspersing me; but I shall return him no other Answer than that of the Mendicant Friar, to some false Accusations against him, *Mentitur impudentissimé.*[6] But sure 'tis much more becoming a Man of Probity to speak openly, and Face to Face, than thus clandestinely to backbite and calumniate.

---

5   This would be Mary, wife of William Herbert, the second Marquess of Powis, who was later implicated in the Jacobite effort to restore a Roman Catholic to the throne of England.

6   "Lie shamelessly"

I have just touch'd upon this Subject, that you may see how much this Narrative will incense the Jesuits against me; but I trust that Providence which so often has deliver'd me out of their Hands, will frustrate all their Designs and Contrivances, that I may say with the Psalmist, He shall reward Evil unto mine Enemies: destroy thou them in thy Truth, Psal. 54. v.5.

I fear this trifling Performance will not be very acceptable to you, because 'tis not so elegant and polite as you perhaps might wish; I was sensible of my own Weakness and Incapacity for it, and therefore depend upon your Goodness to pardon my Errors, and supply my Defects; elegant Expressions, and pomp of Words, are not to be expected from a raw and unpolish'd Japanese. But since I wrote this Treatise in Latine, that it might be afterwards turn'd into English; and oblig'd the Translator to make no Additions or Alterations, 'tis mine, and not his Fault, if you meet with any Imperfections in it.

It was translated out of Latin by Mr Oswald, except from Page 94. to 144. which part I wrote in English, and was prepar'd for the Press by another Hand.

I thought it might not be amiss to begin with an Account of my Travels and Conversion, which will (I hope) afford you some things that are entertaining.

'Tis not my delight, but my grief, that I am obliged to publish my Arguments against those Religions which I could not conform to, because some perhaps will interpret what I have said to reflect upon them; but that was far from my intentions, who only design'd to give you my Reasons why I could not subscribe to them; which if they please not others, yet they do abundantly satisfie me, especially since I as yet was tinctur'd with the Prejudices of the Idolatry I was educated in. Far be it from me to condemn any Man; but as I said before, I only acquaint you, that these things were offensive to me, which perhaps are not so to others.

Now to the Omnipotent and All-wise GOD, I return my most

humble Thanks, who by the assistance of his Holy Spirit, has brought
me to the knowledge of that Religion in which only Salvation is to be
found, and to that Christian Communion which is most conformable
to the Institutions of our Saviour: To whom be all Honour and Praise
now and for ever. Amen.

A
DESCRIPTION
OF THE
Isle FORMOSA.

By Mr. George Psalmanaazaar.

CHAPTER. I

Of the Situation, Magnitude, and Division of the ISLE

THE ISLAND FORMOSA, which by the Natives is called in their Language, Gad Avia, from Gad, Beautiful, and Avia an Isle, and by the Chinese is called Pacando, is one of the most Pleasant and Excellent of all the Asiatick Isles, whether we consider the convenient Situation, the healthful Air, the fruitful Soil, or the curious Springs and useful Rivers, and rich Mines of God and Silver wherewith it abounds; for it enjoys many advantages which other Islands want, and wants none of those which they have.

Formosa and Japan, are the remotest parts towards the East, which are hitherto known or discover'd, and so they are the first Countries that are visited with the Rays of the Morning Sun. Formosa has on the North side Japan, distant about 200 Leagues; on the North and West, China, from which it is distant about 60 Leagues; and on the South side Luconia, from which it is distant about 100 Leagues.

This Isle Formosa extends it self in length from North to South above 70 Leagues, and in breadth from East to West, 15 Leagues, being about 130 Leagues in Circumference. It is divided into five Isles, whereof two are called Avias dos Lardonos, or the Isles of Thieves,[1] the third is called Great Peorko, the fourth Little Peorko, and the fifth, which lies in the middle, and is called Kaboski, or the Principal Island, is greatest of all the five, being 17 Leagues in length and 15 in breadth, is most strictly called Gad Avia, or the Island Formosa; tho' all the rest, which for distinction sake, are called by several Names, are comprehended under the General Name of Formosa; and in this Sense we shall use the Word in the following Account of this Isle.[2]

---

1   Psalmanazar strays closer than usual to reality with his reference to The Isles of Thieves, which was a term used for the Mariana Islands, including Saipan, in the western Pacific to the east of Taiwan. The Spanish called them the Ladrones. But while in the vague vicinity globally speaking, it is still more than 2,500 km from Taiwan to the Marianas. On his fake map, he places The "Isle of Thieves" right next to "Formosa".
2   Great Peorko and Little Peorko could have been inspired by the Pescadores, or Penghu Islands, a group of islands in the Taiwan Strait.

CHAPTER. II

*Of the great Revolutions which have happen'd in the
Island Formosa*

WE FIND IN OUR Chronicles, that above 200 Years ago, the Island
Formosa had been Govern'd for some Ages by one King, who in
his Administration depended upon the Representatives of the
People, who are two or three Men chosen in every City and Village,
to take care of their publick Concerns. This King whom the Natives
in their Language called Bagalo, had one Governor in each of the
aforementioned Isles, subject to his Power, and accountable to him
for their Administration; and this Governor was called by the Natives
Tano. But about 200 Years ago the Emperor of Tartary invaded this
Island and subdued it; which continued under the Dominion of
the Tartars until the third Generation. But the third Emperor who
succeeded after this Conquest, being an Austere Tyranical Prince, who
was very cruel to the Natives, and had formed a design to extirpate
their Religion, did so provoke their natural Rage, that at last they did
all with one consent take up Arms, and rose against his Deputy and
the Forces by which he ruled them, and drove them all out of the
Country, after a bloody Battle. And thus they shook off the Yoke of
Tartarian Bondage, under which they had groan'd above 70 Years, and
restored their Natural Prince to the rightful Throne of his Ancestors,
who now became independent not only of a Foreign Prince, but of all
the little Commonwealths within his own Dominions, in which state
they continued above 70 Years. During which time the Europeans
came thither, viz. the Dutch and English, who maintained a great

Trade with the Natives, especially in Great Peorko, where the Dutch built a Castle called Tyowan. At the same time while the Dutch were there the Chinese came and attempted to land in the Island, with a design to Conquer it, but were stoutly repulsed by the Natives, who took up Arms in defence of their Country, and maintained a War with the Chinese for some Years, until at last they drove them back into their own Country. And the Formosans finding that the Dutch under a false pretence of joining with them to force back the Chinese, had treacherously underhand assisted them to Conquer Formosa, hoping at last to wrest it out of their hands and make it their own; the Hollanders were thereupon banished, and prohibited to come any more into that Island, and their Castle Tyowan was Demolished. Yet upon some fair Promises they were afterwards permitted again to Land there, provided they should stay but a little while, and a sufficient Guard should attend them and observe their Motions. Thither therefore they came, and when they can find what they have a mind to in Formosa, they go no farther; but when they miss of their aim there, then they travel further into Japan, viz. to the Isle of Nangasaque,[3] for they are not permitted to go to any other place. However under these Commotions Formosa still preserved its form of Government independent of a Foreign Prince, until Meryaandanoo first ravished Japan by Villany, and then conquer'd Formosa by a trick, of both which Revolutions I shall now give the Reader a short and true Account, as it is to be found in our Histories, and is firmly believed by all the People of Formosa, upon a constant Tradition from Father to Son, for the space of Fifty Years and upwards.

Meryaandanoo was by Nation a Chinese, but coming to Japan while he was Young, he was by the favour of some Great Man admitted

---

3   In 1634, the Japanese Shogun ordered the construction of an island in the bay by the western city of Nagasaki by the digging of a canal to separate a piece of shore from the mainland, to quarantine foreign traders. In the shape of a fan, the island was called Dejima. The Dutch took it over exclusively in 1641 and operated the trading post until 1853, just a few years before the Americans forced isolationist Japan to open up.

to some mean Office, in the Court of the Emperor Chazadijn, where he continued some time, and had his Education. But the Emperor perceiving that he was a very Ingenious Young-Man, and well qualified for a better Office, gave him at first some inferiour Place in the Army, in which he behaved himself so well, that he was quickly preferr'd to a higher Post, and by his winning behaviour and admirable Conduct, he so far insinuated himself into the favour of the Emperor, that he was gradually advanced from one Post of Honour in the Army to another; until at last he arrived at the highest, and was made Carilhan, or Chief General of all the Imperial Forces, which is the highest Office in the Empire, not only for Honour, but for Power and Trust. And in the administration of this Office, he behaved himself with so much Prudence and Courage, that the Emperor loved him exceedingly; but much more did he win the Heart of the Emperess, who was so taken with his gallant Mien, that she could not live without him. So great was her kindness to him, and she put such an entire confidence in his fair Speeches, that she would often meet him in private places, which was a favour very rare and unusual in that Country, especially from so great a Person as the Emperess. Having thus gained the Love of the Emperor and Emperess, to so great a degree, this ungrateful Villain made use of that familiarity to which the Empress admitted him, and of that confidence they both put in him, first to raise a Jealousie in the Mind of the Emperor against the Emperess; and then by this means to contrive an opportunity for murdering them both, which Barbarous design this Bloody Villain accomplished after this manner. First, he perswaded the Emperor that his Emperess was in Love with a certain Nobleman, whom he supposed, and she often met him, and had private conversation with him in the Garden: Whereupon the Emperor being highly enrag'd both against this Nobleman, whom he falsly accused, and against the Emperess, who was suppos'd to have kept company with him, desired Meryaandanoo to enquire diligently at what Hour, and in what place they were to meet together in the Garden, if it were possible for him to find it out; and then says he, come and acquaint me with it, and I will take care that neither of them shall escape out of my hands, until they have both suffer'd Death, according to the demerit of their Crime. This Meryaandanoo promised to do, as the Emperor had desired him; and sometime after he came out of the Emperor's presence, he went to the Apartment of the Emperess, and having good assurance of her ready compliance, by his former private conversations with her, he pray'd her to meet him, at a certain Hour of that Day, in a certain place of the Garden, which she, mistrusting nothing, readily promised to do, and appointed the time and place for their meeting. Having gained this point, which was a great step towards finishing his design, he went and acquainted the Emperor, that at such an Hour the Nobleman was to come, and to meet his Emperess in such a place of the Garden. Whereupon the Emperor presently commanded his Guards to be got ready with which he intended to seize them both together, and bring them to deserved punishment. In the mean time Meryaandanoo having changed his Clothes, and mask'd his Face, that he might not be known to the Emperor, under this disguise meets the Emperess at the time and place appointed, whom he most Barbarously stabb'd, with a poison'd Dagger, to conceal the Murder, by stopping the Effusion of Blood: The Emperor comes at first all alone into that place of the Garden to satisfie his Curiosity of seeing them together, fearing lest the appearance of the Guards would make them run away; and he perceiv'd a certain Nobleman, as he supposed, lying upon the Emperess in an unseemly posture, he called for his Guards, who were at some distance from the place: But while he advanced towards the Nobleman, not knowing him to be Meryaandanoo, Meryaandanoo was too nimble for him, who came fully prepared to execute the wicked design he had plotted, for he had no sooner called for his Guards, but he closed in with him, and gave him his Deaths wound with the same poison'd Dagger; and immediately after he had struck the blow, he fled away with all possible speed, through unbeaten Paths among

Trees and Bushes, and so made his Escape without being discover'd: When the Guards came and found the Emperor and Emperess both kill'd, they stood for some time astonish'd, at this strange and surprizing Event; but they wonder'd most of all at the Murder of the Emperor, who so lately parted from them, and whom they heard but a little before call upon them to come to him; some condoled the sudden Death of two such great Persons, while others search'd every where about the Garden, among the Trees and Bushes, to find out the Murderer; But when they saw that no discovery could be made, the Soldiers began to Mutiny, had not the Captain of the Guards diverted their Fury, by telling them, That they must do nothing until they had first acquainted the Carilhan with what had happened; whereupon a Party was immediately dispatch'd to his House, (whither he had made his Escape after he had committed the Murder) and when they came there, and told him, he seem'd to be mightily surpris'd and troubl'd, as if he knew nothing of the matter: But to lose no time in a case of so great consequence, he went in all haste to the place, where having viewed the dead Bodies, he express'd his great Sorrow, with many Sighs and Tears, for the loss of two Persons so great and so good, to whom he had been infinitely obliged, and declared that this execrable Murder had been committed by a certain Nobleman, naming him, who had frequently kept Company with the Emperess in private, and had appointed a meeting with her this very Day, as he was well assur'd. This discovery gave great satisfaction to the Guards, who being glad of the opportunity to revenge the Death of their Master, went presently and struck off the Innocent Nobleman's Head, by his Order, who was the Murderer himself. Meryaandanoo having thus far succeeded in his design, wanted now only to be declared Emperor, which met with some opposition from those in the Army, who favoured the Family of Chazadijn, though he had no Children by his Emperess, but only by his Concubines; and for some time there were many Cabals and Factions about the next Successor to the Empire; But at last Meryaandanoo, having pre-engaged a great Party for him, and being generally beloved by the Soldiers, by his prevailing Interest in the Army, was chosen and declar'd Emperor of Japan; which was the finishing of the great design he intended to accomplish, by all the afore-mentioned Villanies and Cruelties.

About two Years after he was promoted to the Imperial Crown of Japan, he counterfeited himself to be sick, and caus'd innumerable Sacrifices to be offered to the Gods of Japan, for the Recovery of his Health; but all these Sacrifices, proving, as he pretended, ineffectual, so that these Gods seem'd either unable or unwilling to relieve him, he declar'd, tho' in deep dissimulation, that it was necessary for him to see for Relief from the Gods of other Countries. And to this end he sent an Ambassadour with a Letter to the King of Formosa, who was to entreat the King of Formosa in his Name, that he might have leave to send and offer Sacrifices to the God of his Country, by whom he hoped to find that cure of his Disease, which in vain he had expected from his own Gods, tho' he had offer'd 10000 Sacrifices to appease them.

His Letter to the King, was to this purpose.

Meryaandanoo, Emperor of Japan, to the King of Formosa, My Friend, &c.

Being afflicted with a very grievous Disease, and having endeavoured by my Oblations to pacifie the Gods of my Country, that I might recover my Health, I have found all my endeavours hitherto ineffectual, whether through the Anger or Impotence of the Gods I know not: And therefore having a great Ventration for your God, of whose great Power and Goodness I am fully perswaded, I must entreat you to give leave that some of my Subjects may be sent into your Island, who shall bring along with them the Beasts they art to offer in Sacrifice to your God, for the Recovery of my Health. And if your God shall be so far appeased by these Sacrifices as to restore me to Health, I do hereby promise you, that through all the Empire of Japan, and in all the other Isles subject to my Dominion, I will plant and establish your Religion. And so your God shall be our God, and we shall live in perpetual Friendship with one another.

I expect your Answer to this Request by my Ambassador.

After the King of Formosa had read the Letter, he sent for his Priests and acquainted them with the Contents of it, and commanded them to consult their God, whether he would grant what the Emperor of Japan had desired: The Priests hoping that they should reap great Profit and Advantage from the Emperor, by the Japannese's coming into their Country, to offer Sacrifice, told the King, that they had consulted their God, and he had consented, that they should come here to offer Sacrifices, but he had not declar'd what success their Oblations should have as to restoring the Health of their Emperor. The King having received this Answer from his Priests, sent for the Ambassadors of the Emperor of Japan, and told them, *Go and salute your Emperor in my Name, and tell him, that he has leave from my God, and from me, to send some of his Subjects to offer Sacrifices to our God; and if our God shall restore his Health, I hope he will perform what he has promised of establishing the Worship of our God in all his Dominions.* The Ambassadors having taken their leave of our King returned home, into their own Country, and acquainted the Emperor of Japan with the Answer of the King of Formosa to his Letter, who was very glad at the good success of their negotiation, having further designs in it than they were aware of. And therefore he presently commanded a great Army to be made ready, and order'd the Soldiers to be put in great Litters, carried by two Elephants, which will hold Thirty, or Forty Men; and to prevent any suspicion of the Formosans, they placed Oxen or Rams to be seen at the Windows of the Litters. Thus he covertly convey'd a numerous Army into the Isle Formosa, with many of the Nobility of his Court, under the Religious pretence of Offering Sacrifice for the Recovery of his Health, but really with a design to Conquer the Country. The numerous Chariots were divided into three parts, the greatest of which were sent into the Capital City Xternetsa, and the two other parts into two other Cities, called Bigno and Khadzey; And at a certain Hour appointed the Chariots were opened in all the three Cities, the Soldiers came out, and with Sword in Hand, threatning present Death to the King, and all the Inhabitants of the City Xternetsa (which was likewise done in the other Cities at the same time) unless they would submit themselves to be governed by the Emperor of Japan. The King considering that he had no other prospect but that of imminent and unavoidable Death before him, and that there was no hopes by his Death to preserve the Ancient Liberties of his Country, chose rather to submit to the fatal necessity he was under, than throw away his Life to no purpose; and the rest of the Inhabitants every where follow'd his example in this surprising danger of Death, so that the whole Kingdom was quickly reduc'd under the Yoke of the Emperor of Japan, without the Effusion of much Blood. And from that time the Emperor of Japan sends a King into the Isle Formosa, who is called Tano Angon, or the superintendent King: But he who was King before, in that Isle, is only a Bagalandro or Viceroy, or one that is next to the King in Dignity without any Power. And this is a short History of the manner how the Isle Formosa was subdued by the Villany of the Emperor Meryaandanoo, who instead of Sacrificing Beasts to the God of the Country, as he pretended, would have Sacrificed the Inhabitants to his own Ambition, if they had not prevented him by a voluntary submission to his Rule and Government. I shall therefore in the next place give an account of the Form of Government in this Isle, which is now almost the same with that which is in the other Isles of *Japan*.

CHAP. III

*Of the Form of Government in the Island Formosa, made
of the New Laws Made by the Emperor Meryaandanoo*

MERYAANDANOO BEING thus settled Emperor of Japan and Formosa,
made new Laws relating to the Deputy King, and enforced the old
Laws relating to the Subjects, with grievous Penalties, as will appear
hereafter.

The First Law is, Concerning the Kings that are subject to him,
who are Twenty Five in number (besides the Eight who are not
properly called Angons or Bagalos but Viceroys or Bagelanders)
And these Kings are oblieged, by this Law, twice in a Year to wait
upon the Emperor, and then every one of them is to give an account
of his Administration of the Government, and of all the Notable
Occurrences which have happened in his Kingdom for the space of
half a Year, and to receive the new Commands of the Emperor, if he
shall think fit to give any.

The Second Law is, That none of them shall transgress the
Commands of the Emperor, unless he first acquaints him with the
necessity that forces him to do it; yet in a case of urgent necessity, this
Law is moderated by Equity.

The Third Law is, That they shall do nothing to the detriment
of the People, subject to their Government; That they shall not be
unjust, or cruel, to them, or any ways prejudice them in their Life,
Fortune, or Reputation, without a just cause: which Law he made to
gain the Love of the People.

The Fourth is, That none of the Kings shall suffer a Christian to live in his Country, but every one of them shall keep Searchers, or Centinels in the several Sea Ports, who shall Try all Foreigners, as soon as they arrive in the Harbour whether they be Christians or no, by this Test, of trampling upon the Crucifix; which Test was chiefly design'd against the Papists, who worship the Crucifix, and therefore dare not trample upon it: But as to other Foreigners who do trample upon the Crucifix, the Governour is to grant them a Pass to Travel through all the Cities under his Dominion, provided they are not above Twenty in number.

The last is, That no King can prohibit or enjoin any Religion, in his Country, but every subject shall enjoy the Liberty of his Conscience to worship his God after his own way, except there shall be any found that are Christians; for the discovery of whom there shall be Searchers appointed in all Cities and Villages, who shall try them by the Test aforementioned, And to all these Laws this Sanction is added, That if any Person shall violate any one of these Laws they shall presently be put to Death, which is the true Reason, why the Commands of the Emperor are every where so exactly obey'd.

He made no new Laws relating to the Subjects, but only revived the Natural and Ancient Laws, which he enforced with new Penalties proportionable to the Crimes.

The First is against the Christians, That if any Foreigner shall be found who is a Christian, and who hath seduc'd or endeavoured to seduce the Inhabitants to Christianity, he shall be imprison'd, together with all those whom he hath seduced, And if he will Renounce the Christian Faith, and worship Idols, he shall not only be pardon'd, but have a certain Pension allowed him for his Subsistence; but if he refuse to do this, he shall be burnt alive; And as to those who have been seduc'd, if they will return to their former Idolatry, they shall be set at liberty; but if they will not, they shall be hang'd.

The Second is against Murderers, Thieves and Robbers, viz. Whosoever shall kill another Man unjustly, shall be hang'd up by the

Feet with his head downward, and after this manner shall hang alive a longer or shorter time, according to the aggravation of his Crime, until he be shot to Death with Arrows: But if he be both a Robber and a Murderer he shall be Crucified, A Thief shall be punished according to the heinousness of his Crime, either with Hanging, or continual Imprisonment, or with Whipping, or a Fine.

The Third Law is against Adulterers, viz. They shall for the first Offence pay a Fine of 100 Copans (each Copan being a piece of Gold weighing a Pound) and those who have not Money to pay such a Fine, they shall be publickly Whipt by the Hand of the Hangman. But if any Person be guilty of the same Crime a second time, he or she shall be beheaded. For though, as will appear in the following Chapter about Religion, every Man may have as many Wives, as his Estate is able to maintain; yet if any Man shall carnally know another Woman besides his own Wives, to whom he has promised Fidelity, he is guilty of Adultery. The same Law obliges all those who are unmarried provided they be Natives of the Country: But this Law does not extend to Foreigners, to whom the Natives are wont to offer Virgins or Whores, to be made use of at their Pleasure, with Impunity.

But here I must desire the Reader to observe, that the Husband has such full power over his Wife, that if he apprehend her in the act of Adultery; he may punish her after what manner, and to what degree he pleases, even unto Death: But if the thing be not commonly known, he may spare her, if he thinks fit, upon her promise of amendment for the future.

The Fourth Law is, Whosoever shall Suborn false Witness against any Man, both he and the false Witnesses shall have their Tongue cut out, and be further punish'd according to the heinousness of the Crime, and the damage done to the Party, against whom they testified.[4]

---

4   There is an echo in Psalmanazar's fantasy construction of Formosan religion of the accounts of Aztec human sacrifices as described by the Spanish conquistadors.

The Fifth Law is, Whosoever shall blaspheme the God of the Country he shall be burnt alive. The Sixth is, If a Son or a Daughter shall strike their Father or Mother, or one of their Kindred that is Ancient, or one that is superiour to them in Power, their Arms and Legs shall be cut off, and a Stone being tied about their Neck, they shall be thrown into the Sea, or a River. But if any one shall strike a Priest, their Arms shall be burnt off, and then their Body shall be buried alive.

Whosoever shall strike his King, Intendant or Governour, shall be hang'd up by the Feet till he die, having four Dogs fasten'd to his Body to tear it in pieces.

The Seventh is, Whosoever shall Reproach or Slander any Man, shall have his Tongue bored through with a hot Iron: But whosoever refuses to obey his Superiour in things Lawful, shall be beheaded.

The Eighth is, Whosoever shall Plot any Treason against the Emperor, or any of the Kings, or shall endeavour the Subversion of the Religion establish'd, he shall be tortur'd with all imaginable Torments.

All these Laws Meryaandanoo made, or revived in the fourth Year of his Empire, at a meeting of all the Kings of his Empire, and of all the chief Priests of every City. And by vertue of them, all the Inhabitants enjoy a profound Peace; for as the Subjects do readily obey the Laws relating to themselves, so the Governours and Officers are careful to put them in Execution whenever there is occasion.

This is what I chiefly intended in this Chapter, to give an account of the Laws and their Sanctions, by which Meryaandanoo governs his Deputy-Kings and their Subjects; and though there are other things which might be placed here under this head of Government, yet because they are hereafter to be inserted in their proper places, they are here omitted.

CHAP. IV

Of the Religion of the Formosans

SINCE MY DESIGN is only to give an account of the Isle Formosa, I shall briefly mention but three kinds of Religion that are observed in Japan, because of the Affinity some of them have with that which is established in Formosa.[5]

The First kind of Religion is Idolatry, or the Worship of Idols: And this kind of Worship most generally prevails above all others in Japan, so that in one Temple call'd Amida, in the Capital City of Meaco, there are no fewer than 3500 Idols; whereof 1000 are of Gold, 1000 of Silver, and 1000 of Brass, and 500 of Wood and Stone, and to these Idols they Sacrifice Oxen, Rams, Goats, and such like Beasts, and some times they Sacrifice Infants to them, when their God is not appeased by other Sacrifices.

The second kind of Religion, is that of those who acknowledge one God, whom they believe to be so Sublime and Great, that they dare not Sacrifice to him; and therefore they have establish'd the Sun as the great Power of God which Rules and Governs the World, and the Moon and Stars as powers inferior to the Sun, which more exactly inspect and take care of Terrestial affairs: Wherefore they

---

5   His description of the rules governing Christians are a mangled version of the reality of Christianity in Japan. The real history is that the Jesuit priest Francis Xavier and three Japanese converts arrived in Japan in 1549 to start the process of converting Japan to Catholicism. The ruling Japanese Shogunate decided in the late 16th century that Christianity was a threat and worked to weed it out. Most famously 26 Christians who refused to renounce the religion were crucified in Nagasaki in 1597.

The Dutch, from their outposts on the coast of Taiwan, also engaged in vigorous evangelical activities, proselytysing the Taiwan population.

Sacrifice Infants to the Sun, and Beasts to the Moon and Stars.

The Third sort is rather a Sect of Atheism than Religion, for they deny the being of God, and affirm that the World was from Eternity and shall continue to Eternity. Hence some of them think that the Soul is Mortal and dies with the Body, like that of Beasts; but others of them say that the Soul is not Mortal, but informs another Body after Death, and so it passes out of one Body into another to Eternity. Whensoever the Soul has done well, they think it passes into the Body of a Rich man who lives in great ease and pleasure, but if it has done evil it passes into the Body of some poor Wretch to suffer Pain and Misery; and so the Soul is liable to endless Vicissitudes of Vertue and Vice, of pleasure and Pain, These Atheists use no Religious Worship, saving that they all offer Sacrifice to evil Spirits or Devils, that they may not hurt them. But the Transmigration of Souls, is believ'd not only by them but by all the Jappannese, except those who think that the Soul is Mortal.

But my business is not to give a particular account of their several opinions, and different ways of Worship, and therefore I have noted these things only en passant to show wherein they agree, and wherein they differ from the Religion establish'd in Formosa.

The Religion of the Formosans was reveal'd by their God, if we may believe their Jarhabadiond (i.e. the Election of the Land) which makes mention of the Revelation upon which they found the Religious Worship now us'd among them, and gives the following account of it: That about 900 Years ago, the Inhabitants of Formosa knew no other Gods but the Sun and the Moon, whom they believed to be Supreme, and the Stars, which they looked upon to be as it were Semidei, or Subordinate Gods; and then their whole Worship consisted in adoring them Morning and Evening, and offering them the Sacrifices of Beasts, But after some time there arose two Philosophers, who had led a Pious and Austere kind of Life in the Deserts, and pretended that God had appear'd to them, and spoke to them, to this purpose; I am much Troubled for the Blindness of this People because they Worship the Sun, Moon and Stars so devoutly, as the Supreme Deity; go and tell them, I am the Lord of the Sun, Moon and Stars, of the Heaven, the Earth, the Sea and all things that are in them, I Govern the Creatures by the Sun and Moon and the 10 Stars, and without me they cannot exist: Go and tell them, that God has appear'd to you, and said, if they will worship and adore him, he will be their Protector, and will appear to them in the Churches, which they Build to his honour, and promise them in my Name, that if they Worship and obay me, they shall receive great rewards after this Life. The Names of these two Philosophers, were Zeroaboabel, which is a Name unknown to the Japannese, and Chorhe Mathcin, which in the Japan Language signifies Creator Annunciat, for Chorhe signifies the Creator, and Mathcin declares. Now these two pretending that God had spoke to them, came to a certain Mountain call'd Tanalio near the Capital City, where the People were met together to offer Sacrifice to the Sun, and told them to this Effect. O ye Blind Mortals, who Worship the Stars so devoutly, and are ignorant of the God who is above them; that God who Created the Sun and Moon, and all things in Heaven and Earth, has this day taken pity on you, and appeared to us, and commanded us to declare him unto you: And after they had said this, they Demonstrated by many Arguments, that there is one Supreme God, who is above all the visible things in this World. This discourse so much affected the People, that they desired to know of them, how that God would be Worshiped, whether they should Worship him after the same manner, as they now Worshiped the Sun. To which they answered, no. But if they would Worship him according to his mind, in an acceptable manner, they should first Build him a Temple, and in that they should make a Tabernacle, and an Altar, and upon the Altar they should Burn 20000 Hearts of young Children, under 9 Years of Age. And when ye have done these things, said they, then God will appear to you in this Tabernacle, and tell you what you are to do further for his Service. When the People heard these things, they could no longer refrain themselves, but exclaimed against these two Prophets, as Hypocrites and Impostors; and asked them in great rage, how can your God be so Cruel as to require us to kill so many of our Sons, and offer them up in Sacrifice to him: Whereupon the two Prophets fled away into the Desert again, having left these Threatning words behind them, We have told you what our God Commanded us to say unto you; but if ye will not believe our words, and obey his will, ye shall quickly find, that the Divine Vengeance will pursue you.

A little while after it was observ'd, that the Sky was Darkned, there fell much Rain with Hail, which destroyed the Fruits of the Ground, innumerable claps of Thunder were heard in the Air, there were great Earth-quakes in several places, and the Air became so Pestilential, that the greatest part of the Inhabitants were visited with the Plague, the wild Beasts came into their Cities, and even into their Houses, and devoured their young Children: And these Calamities lasted for a day and a half, which were so Terrible, that the whole Island seemed to be in danger of utter Ruin and Destruction. Which sad Prospect moved all the Inhabitants to return Unanimously to the Mountain aforesaid, and there they confessed their great fault in refusing to believe the two Prophets, and cry'd earnestly with all their Hearts to that God, who had spoken to them by those Prophets, deprecating his Wrath for their past Offences, and Promising they would do whatsoever he should command them if he would now spare them. And at length, after long and humble Supplication, that God sent them a Prophet, which should declare a new Peace and Reconciliation between him and them, upon which account they called him Psalmanaazaar, i.e. the Author of Peace, After he had Published this joyful Message unto them, he commanded them to build a Temple, and in it an Alter, above that Alter to make a Tabernacle, and then to Sacrifice upon the Alter, 100 oxen, 100 Rams

A Temple

and 100 Goats, and to Burn upon it 20000 Hearts of young Children under 9 Years of Age, and then God would appear to them: They built therefore a Temple, after the form described in the First Figure.

The first Figure explained

A.   The Tower in which God appears in the Tabernacle.

B.   The Tower in which are the Singers and Players upon Instruments.

C.   The Window-Tower, which lets in the Sky-light.

D.   The Head of an Oxe, or a Symbol of God.

E.   An Image of the Sun.

F.   An Image of the Moon.

G.   The Gate of the Temple.

H.   The Windows.

I.   The parts cover'd with Gold.

K.   The place for the Men.

L.   The place for the Women.

The whole Temple is built of Four-square Stones after an exact Model, and is a most Finish'd piece of Architecture, being of great Bigness and Height. In the Tower which looks towards the East is the Tabernacle, wherein God appears, and the Altar; all which they built by the Command of the Prophet P1almanaazaar.

The Second Figure explained

1. A Crown hanging from the Roof over the top of the Tabernacle. 2. The Head of an Oxe, or the Symbol of their God. 3. The top of the Tabernacle with 5 burning Lamps. 4. A little Pyramid upon which is the Figure of the Sun. 5. Another upon which is the Figure of the Moon. 6. A Lamp to the honour of the Moon. 7. A Lamp to the honour of the Sun. 8. 8. 2 Curtains which cover the Concavity of the Tabernacle on the Ordinary days. 9. The Concavity of the Tabernacle adorned with a Sky-colour and Stars of Gold, representing the

Firmament, in which God appears. 10. Their God showing himself to the People, in the shape of an Ox. 11. 11. Two Lamps burning to the honour of their God.

12.12. Two Pyramids upon which are the 10 Stars, which are Worshiped. And all these things are to be made of Gold or Silver. 13. The Gridiron upon which the hearts of the young Children are burnt. 14.14. The Furnace of Fire for burning them. 15.15. The Chimneys by which the Smoke goes out. 16. The Caldron in which the Flesh of the Sacrifice is boyled. 17.17. The Furnace of Fire for boyling them. 18. The Sanctuary, or the place in which the young Children are Slain. 19. The pit in which their Blood and Bodies are placed. 20. The holy place wherein the Beasts are Slain for Sacrifice. 21. A Marble-structure in which is a Gridiron. 22. A Stone-structure that encompasseth the Caldron in the form of an Altar. 23. The smoke of a Furnace. 24. The round part of the Roof; 25. the Wall.

This is the Figure of the Tabernacle, (as the first was of the Temple) which Psalmanaazaar, Commanded to be built.

The first Temple was built in the Capital City Xternetsa, and the Tabernacle was plac'd in it. And after these were Finish'd, every Magistrate in the several Cities and Villages, took an account how many Sons there were in each Family, that they might be obliged to Furnish their Proportion for the Sacrifices, that were to be offered to this new God, according to the Number of Sons that was in every Family. All things being thus prepared a great Festival of 10 days was Celebrated and every day of the 10, 2000 Infants were Sacrificed: And then after the Festival was ended, and the last Sacrifice was offer'd, their new God begun to appear in the shape of an Oxe, and spoke to the People, and to Psalmanaazaar, and dictated to him whatever he would have done to his honour.

He said therefore ye shall divide the Year into 10 Months, which ye shall call by the Names of the 10 Stars, viz. *Dig, Damen, Analmen, Anioul, Dattibes, Dabes, Anaber, Nechem, Koriam, Turbam*. Every Month shall have four weeks, and five of these Months shall have 37 days, viz. the first, 3d. 5th. 7th. and 9th, the other 5 shall have only 36 days, Every week shall have 9 days, but in the Months which have 37 days, the last week shall have 10 days, and the 10th. shall be a day of Fasting.

Ye shall begin the Year from this day, which is the first day of the Month Dig, and the first of the Festival of 10 days, and at this Festival ye shall Sacrifice to me every Year the hearts of 18000 young Boys, under the Age of 9 Years, on the first day of the Year Every Month ye shall Sacrifice in all your Temples 1000 Beasts, viz. 300 Bulls, 400 Sheep or Rams, and the rest in Calves or Lambs: and every Parish shall Furnish their proportion for these Sacrifices, according to their ability. Every week ye shall offer of Fowls as you are able, and all these Things you shall carefully observe every Year.

Of the Festivals

Ye shall celebrate Two great Festivals to my Honour, the First at the beginning of the new Year, which shall fast for a whole Week, and the Second in the last Week of the 5th Month, which shall also last for Nine Days. The first and last of these Days shall be observ'd by rising early in the Morning and Adoring, and after ye have worshipp'd, ye shall come into the Temple, and Pray and Sing Hymns from One a Clock until Two: At Two a Clock ye shall go to a Fountain or River without the City, and there ye shall throw Water upon your Head twelve Times, and then ye shall return into the Temple, ye shall go and return all together, and while ye are on the way which shall take up the space of an Hour in going and returning, ye shall be all the while Praying. And after ye are return'd, then the Beasts shall be slain, and divided into parts, and purified, and boil'd in their Blood; and every one shall come before the Altar, and take a Piece of the Flesh from the Hand of the Priest, and shall eat it, bending his left Knee and bowing his Head down to the Ground; and during all that time the Instruments of Musick shall Play, and the Singing Men and all the People present shall sing Hymns together. The time of slaying and offering the Sacrifices shall last for three Hours, viz. from three a Clock till Six, and at Six there shall be a Sermon, or an Explication of the first Principles of Religion, and then a Thanksgiving, which being ended, ye shall return Home, and continue there Eating and Drinking until the second Hour. After which ye shall return to the Temple again, and continue there until the sixth Hour, Praying and Singing, with the Instruments of Musick playing; and then there shall be again a Lecture upon the Catechetical Doctrins, which being ended, ye shall return Home and recreate your selves with any lawful Diversions.

On other Days, between the first and last of the Month, ye shall rise in the Morning and Worship, ye shall throw Water upon your Head three times, and then go to the Temple and stay there from the first Hour to the sixth. After the sixth ye shall return Home, and then ye may follow any lawful Employment.

But here the Reader is desir'd to take notice, That the Day with them is divided into four Parts, and each Part into six Hours; when therefore it is said, They shall stay in the Temple from the first Hour to the sixth, it is to be understood they shall stay from 6 a Clock to according to the way of reckoning Time us'd in Europe.

Ye shall call the first and last Day of the Festival a double Feast, and the other Days simple Feasts. On the first Day of the Month ye shall celebrate a double Feast, and on the second a simple Feast, and ye shall Sacrifice Oxen and Sheep, &c. and ye shall Eat of them. The first Day of the Week shall be a double Feast, and ye shall Sacrifice Fowls and eat of them.

Note, That a Festival is therefore call'd double, because the People go twice to the Temple on that Day, and it is call'd simple because they go but once.

And further it is to be noted, that instead of the Clocks us'd in

80

Europe, they measure Time by an Instrument made of Wood, in the form of an Hour Glass, which being fill'd with Sand, runs all out in the space of an Hour: And this being observ'd by certain Watchmen appointed on purpose for that end, as soon as the Sand is run out, they beat a Drum, and give notice what Hour it is, which is the Custom us'd in all Cities, but the Country People judge as exactly as they can what Hour it is by the Sun Moon or Stars.

CHAP. V
Of Fasting-Days

THEIR GOD SAID moreover to Psalmanaazaar; Besides those 5 Days aforesaid, ye shall observe 2 Fasts: The first shall be in the last Week of the Year, which shall last for 8 Days, and it shall be a Preparation for the New Year: The second shall be in the third Week of the fifth Month, and it shall also last for eight Days. On these Fasting-Days, ye shall neither Eat nor Drink any thing until the Sun sets, but after it is set, every one may Eat and Drink to the full until he satiate himself. On these Fasting-Days ye may Pray to me, but on your common Days ye shall not dare to adore me. These Fasts shall be observ'd after this manner, When ye rise in the Morning ye shall Worship, and then wash your Head and Hands and Feet, and after that every one shall employ himself in some lawful Business; but neither you nor your Cattel shall Eat or Drink any thing all that Day until the Sun set. These Fasts shall be every Year observ'd as they are prescrib'd: And indeed they are so rigorously observ'd, that a Man would sooner Die for Thirst then taste a drop of Water on these Days; and all the Cattle are shut up in such Places, where they have nothing to eat all Day; and all Eatables are laid up where they cannot be seen, lest any one should be tempted to break the Fast: In fine, these are true Fasts and strictly kept, as far as human frailty will permit, and not like the Fasts of the Papists, wherein they can Feast upon Fish and Wine.

CHAP. VI

Of the Ceremonies to be observ'd on Festival-Days

ON THE DOUBLE Festivals the People wash their Head, Hands and Feet, and then they go to the Temple, where the Jarhabadiond is publickly read before them all by one of the Priests; and after that is Read, they all of them fall prostrate on the Ground, and the Priests return Thanks to their God with a loud Voice, who of his infinite Mercy has call'd them to the true Knowledge of himself, the People in the mean time joyning in their Hearts with the Words of the Priest. After the Thanksgiving the People rise up, and some Hymns made by the Chief Priests are sung, the Flute and Tymbrel and other Instruments of Musick playing all the while: Then the Priests begin to pray for the Sanctification of the Victims, and after that they slay them and receive the Blood into a Copper; they divide the Flesh into Pieces, and then Boil it with the Blood in a Chaldron which is upon the Altar; while the Flesh is a Boiling, the Chief Priest Prays to God, that he would be pleas'd to accept of these Sacrifices for the Remission of idle Sins of the People: And after the Flesh is Boil'd, the People draw near before the Altar, and cry one of them receives a piece of it from the Hand of the Priest, bowing down his Head when he takes it, and all this time the rest are Singing, and the Instruments of Musick playing. After these Ceremonies are ended, a Priest goes up to a Place higher than the Seats of the People, and there he Preaches and instructs the People, who ask him Questions, and he answers them. At last Thanks are return'd, and Prayers are made for all Things necessary, and then all the People go Home to Dinner, where they are to continue only for the space of two Hours, which is all the time allow'd them between Morning and Evening Service, during which time they must not indulge themselves to excess, or do any thing that's unlawful, but behave themselves very modestly; and then they return to the Temple, where the same Ceremonies are us'd as were in the Morning, except the Sacrifices; and the Service being ended they go to their own Houses, and after Supper they may Walk, Play, or use any other lawful Recreation; but they must not do any servile Work on that Day.

Simple Festivals are celebrated after the same manner as the Vespers of the double Festivals.

It is further to be remarked, That on Festival Days, after the Sacrifice is ended, and the Tabernacle in which their God dwells is open'd, when God appears in the form of a Lyon, or a Bear, or some other fierce Beast, that then God is thought to be Angry with the People: And therefore in such a Case the Tabernacle is to be shut up again, and new Sacrifices of Beasts are to be offer'd, until God shall appear in another Shape, viz. of an Ox, a Calf, a Lamb, or such like Beasts: And if these Sacrifices of Beasts are not sufficient to change the angry God into another shape, then Infants are to be offer'd in Sacrifice unto him, until such time as, their God appearing in 'another form, shows himself to be pacified and reconcil'd unto the People: And if at any time he appears in the form of an Elephant, then we hope that he will do great Things for us. The Priests are to prepare themselves by Fasting and Prayer, before they presume to speak to God in secret, and after they have been with him, they declare to the People what he says.

'Tis yet further to be noted, That their God always assumes the shape of a masculine Creature, and never of a Female, from whence they have been induc'd to believe, that a Woman is so impure, that she can never attain to Happiness, until she be Transform'd into the Body either of Man, or some Male Beast.

CHAP. VII

Of the Election of Priests

AFTER THIS, THEIR God spoke to Psalmanaazaar, and said, you shall choose one Priest, who shall preside over all the rest in the whole Isle, and he shall give Power to others to exercise the Priestly Office. This High-Priest shall never Marry a Wife while he continues in his Office, but if his Constitution obliges him to Marry, then the other Priests shall choose another in his room, and he shall resign his Office, and Marry when he pleases: The other inferior Priests may marry and keep one Wife, except they be Regulars; and then they are oblig'd to continue unmarried, and to live in Convents with their Brethren under one Superior, who shall admit them to the Priestly Office. But if these Regulars also should have a violent Inclination to marry, then they must first leave the Convent, and resign their Office, and after that they may marry. The Office of these Regulars, is to instruct the Youth in the Principles of their Religion, to teach them to Read and Write, and whatsoever else may conduce to their Edification. Besides, these Regulars are oblig'd to lead Religious Lives, and to Cloath themselves in distinguishing Habits; they are to shave their Head, but not to cut their Beard. They are to wear a Gown that does not open before or behind, and a Hood upon their Heads: And lastly, they may retire from the World, and live in desert Places, if they think fit to choose such an austere kind of Life.

As their God had Commanded, so did Psalmanaazaar. He created one ancient Philosopher of the Royal Progeny High-Priest, to whom he gave the power of ordaining all the other inferior Priests.

This High-Priest therefore chose three out of the Citizens of every City, whom he ordain'd Priests, and one in every Village, until such time as Temples were every where built: And then the number of Priests was more encreas'd insomuch that in the City Xternetsa the number grew at last to 160, and was proportionably augmented in other places, whether Cities or Villages. Pialmanaazaar establish'd also a Monastery in Xternetsa, and in many other Cities, in which the Regulars were to live according to the Rules abovemention'd, which were prescrib'd by their God. Lastly he gave order, That this High-priest should ordain in every City one Priest, who might ordain others; and he was call'd the Chief Sacrificator, and has the power to ordain other subordinate Priests and Sacrificators. These are the Rites and Ceremonies deliver'd to the Formosans from their God, by his Prophet Palmanaazaar, which have been ever since observed in their Country.

Now the Names of all the several kinds of Priests in our Language are these: The High priest is call'd Gnotoy Bonzo, the Chief Sacrificator is call'd Gnotoy Tarhadiazar; the inferior Sacrificators, are called Os Tarhadiazors; the Priests who read the Book of the Law and the Prayers, are call'd Ches Bonzos. The secular Priests are call'd Bonzos Leydos, and the Regular Bonzos Roches, and the Superior who is set over the Regulars is call'd Bonzo Soulleto; the Masters who teach the young Children, are call'd Gnosophes Bonzos, and lastly the Preachers are call'd Bonzos Jatupinos.

The Office of the High-priest is to ordain others, to speak to God in private, and declare his Will to all the other Priests, and to chastise those who do not faithfully discharge their Office.

The Office of the Chief-Sacrificator is to ordain other Priests within his own Precinct, which is as it were his Diocese, to rule over them, and to take care: of the Sacrifices, but chiefly of the Infants that are to be Sacrific'd; for which end he: is to take an account how many Boys each Family can furnish, and to admonish them in time to send in their number.

Moreover he alone is to cut the Throats of the Infants, and pluck out their Hearts; others are to lay them upon the Gridiron, but he is to Pray publickly all the time they are a Burning.

The Office of the Subordinate Sacrificators, is to slay the Beasts, to wash and Boil them, and distribute pieces of their Flesh to the People; and some of them are oblig'd to pray with the High priest all the time that these things are a doing.

The Office of the secular Priests is various, for some of them are Readers, others Preachers, or Instructors of Youth, and others of them look after the Temple and Tabernacle, to see that all the Utensils belonging to them be kept in good Order.

The regular Priests, as I have already told you, use to instruct Youth, and to Preach; but moreover they should live retir'd from the World, preserve Chastity, and continue in Celibacy; they should submit themselves to their superiors, fast once a Week, and by all means improve in Vertue. But if once they be debauch'd, they do no longer observe the Rule deliver'd as they believe, by their God, and their Ancestors.

And here it is to be noted, That these Regulars do not make such Vows as the Popish Monks do; for they only take the Vow of Celibacy, neither do they Vow That so absolutely, but that they are still left at liberty, if they find that they cannot refrain from Women, to leave the Monastery, and then to marry a Wife. But they make no Vows of a blind obedience to their Superiors, of an affected poverty, and Humility, and of renouncing the Riches of this World. The only general Law of these Societies is this, whosoever finds himself fit and disposed to embrace a retir'd kind of Life, provided he be Pious, Learned and sincere, whether he be Rich or Poor, is to be admitted into a Convent, and when he enters, he is to bring with him that part of his Fathers Estate that belongs to him, and add it to the Revenues of the Convent. But if he be oblig'd, out of a desire of Marrying, to leave it, then all the Goods he brought with him into the Convent are restored to him, and necessary Food and Raiment are gratis given him, while he continued in it. But if he require any thing extra ordinary, over and above the common allowance of the Convent, as some do, then this is to be Furnished at his own proper Charge, yet he is never permitted to go out of the bounds of the Convent, until he leave it for good and all. If any one die in the Convent, he is to leave all his Goods to it, and while he lives in it, he is to obey his Superior in all things which concern their Rules, but no further. For if any Superior should command one of the Regulars to Eat only Roots, while others fare Deliciously, he may refuse to obey him. But this is a Case that has never happen'd. Thus all Religious Rites and Ceremonies, are Administered by one High-Priest, by some Sacrificators, and some that are Subordinate to them, and by Regular and Secular Priests. But because all that has been hitherto said, relates only to the Worship of their God, we shall now add something concerning the way of Worshipping the Sun, Moon and Stars, which are their Ancient Visible Deities.

CHAP. VIII

Concerning the Worship of Sun, Moon and Stars

MOREOVER THE GOD of Formosa said unto Psalmanaazaar, it shall not be Lawful for you on common days to invoke or worship me, but only the Sun, Moon and 10 Stars, which I have appointed Governors to Rule the World, and to provide all things necessary for you, and ye shall Sacrifice the same Beasts to them as ye do to me, but none of your Infants shall be offered up in Sacrifice to them, for this is my peculiar Worship, which belongs to me only: And after this manner ye shall Worship and adore them.

In the Morning, at the first hour, at least on the common days, ye shall rise up, and throw Water thrice upon your Head, and then ye shall ascend to the Roof of your House, and there ye shall adore the Sun and 5 Stars, and pray to them, not for any thing in particular, but only in general, that they would grant you such things as they know to be necessary for you, and return them thanks for the Favours ye have formerly Receiv'd from them. And in the night time, at the first hour ye shall Worship the Moon and the other five Stars, after the same manner. For ye must know that the Sun is the first and most excellent Creature, which I have Created to govern you, and to him I have given power of conferring Benefits upon you, according as you deserve well of me and him. The Moon I have plac'd in the next degree below him, and the 10 Stars likewise in their proper Places, as being Inferior to the other two. But if ye neglect to Worship them, I have given them power not only to keep back the good things they can bestow, but also to do you mischief, by afflicting your Bodies with Grievous diseases, by destroying the Fruits of your Ground, and Poysoning the Air you Breath with Pestilential Vapors: And therefore ye shall account it your daily Duty, on the common days to Worship and Adore them, after the manner afore prescribed: Moreover ye shall observe three Festivals in the Year, one to the honour of the Sun, another to the honour of the Moon, and a Third to the Honour of the 10 Stars. The First shall be in the First week of the Second Month called Damen, and shall last from the Third until the Ninth day of the week. The Second shall be in the First week of the 5th. Month called Dattibes, and shall last from the Third unto the 9th, day of the week. The 2d, shall be in the Third week of the 8th. Month called Koriam, and shall last from the 5th. to the 9th. day of the week.

Ye shall make choice of a Mountain on which ye shall build three Alters, one to the honour of the Sun, another to the honour of the Moon, and the 3d. to the honour of the 10 Stars. Every City shall choose such a Mountain to itself, in some place near adjoyning, in which all the Citizens and Country-men shall meet together on the First and last day of their Festival, and there ye shall Sacrifice the same Number of Beasts as ye do to me. Ye shall not Eat of the Flesh of them, but consume it wholly in the Fire, and every one shall carry home with him part of the Ashes. During all these Festival days ye shall not Work at your ordinary Trades; but after the Sacrifice is ended, ye may use any lawful Recreation. The Sacrifice shall begin at the 2d. hour in the Morning, and shall last until the 6th: But at night, every Family, shall Worship on the Top of their House, as they use to do on the common days, the Sun, Moon and Stars, at least all of them together. On the days between the first and last of the Festival ye shall go to the Mountain, not to offer Sacrifice there, but for Adoration, and then ye shall Sing and Play upon Instruments of Musick. The High Priest shall take care to appoint other Priests to do Sacrifice to them, they are employ'd to offer Sacrifice to me; And these Priests shall have leave to keep 2 Wives and no more.

These Rules of worship Psalmanaazaar delivered as from our God to the People, whereupon the Citizens of every City built 3 Altars upon a Mountain, after the fashion represented in the following Figure.

The Third Figure explained
1. The Image of the Sun, 2. 2. Two Pots of Incense, wherein Incense is burnt before the Sun on its Feast Days. 3. The top of the Altar. The Altar. 5. The Holy Place in which the Beasts are slain. 6. The Place in which they are burnt. 7 and 8. 8, 8. The Stone-wall wherewith it is encompass'd.

The Fourth Figure explain' d
The Image of the Moon. b. two Incense pots smoking on the Festival Days. c. the top of the Altar. D. the Altar. e. the Holy Place wherein the Beasts are slain. F. the Place where they are burnt. g. g. the Wall that encompasses the Altar.

The Fifth Figure explain'd
A. Dig. B. Damen. C. Analmen. D. Anioul. E. Dattibt1. F. Dabe1. G. Anaber. H. Nechem, I. Koriam. K. Turbam. which are the Names of the Stars that are ador'd. L. the top of the Altar. M.M. two Incense-pots. N. the Altar. O. the Holy Place in which the Beasts are slain. P. The Place in which they are burnt. Q.Q. the Wall.

Let us suppose then that the Paper is the Mountain, on the top of it is built an Altar to the Sun, and in a Place a little below that, is built one to the Moon, and in a Place yet lower, there is one to the 10 Stars.

Thus the People did punctually obey the Commands of our God, and his Orders as to Religious Worship, are strictly observ'd to this very Day.

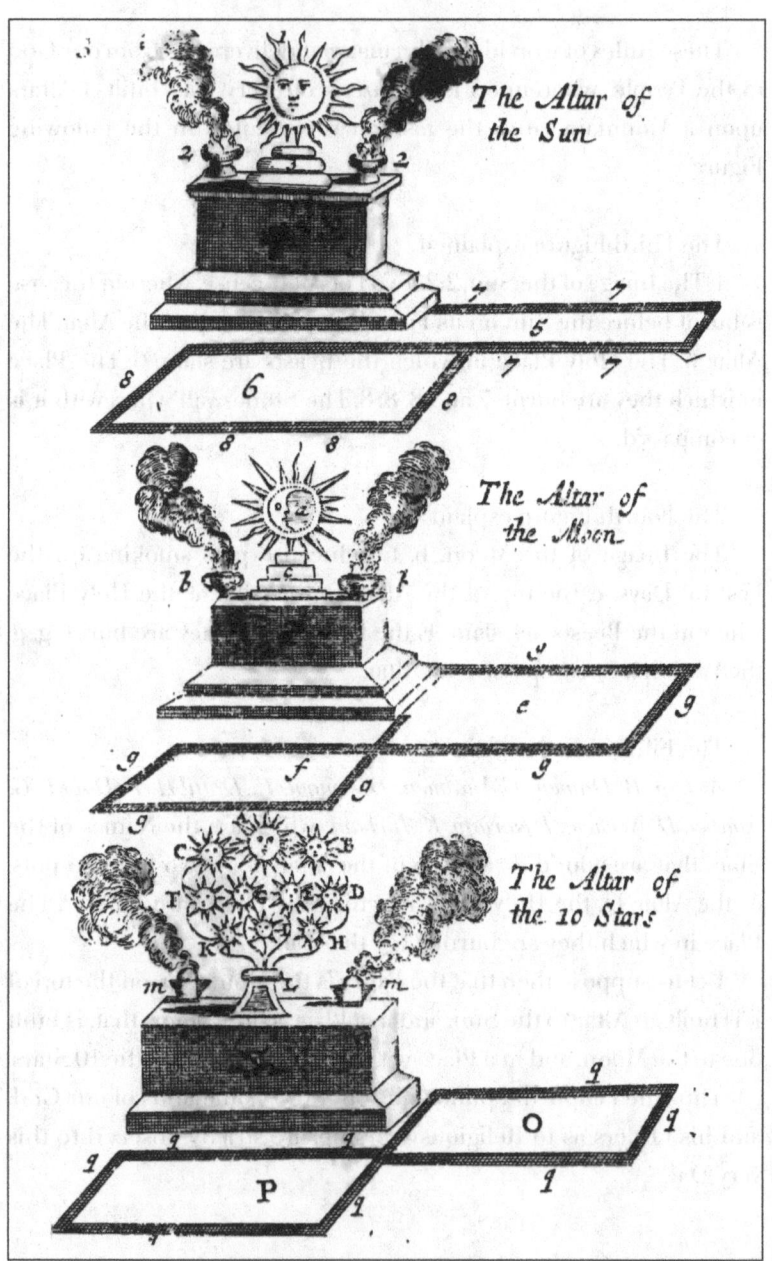

CHAP. IX

Of the Postures of the Body in Adoring

THE FORMOSANS in Adoring God, use various Postures of Body according to the several Parts of Religious Worship they are performing: For 1st, When the Jarhabadiond is publickly read in their Temples, every one of them, at least if he be capable of doing it, bends a little the right Knee, and lifts up the right Hand towards Heaven. 2. When Thanks are given to God, then all of them fall prostrate on the Ground. 3. After the Thanksgiving, when they Sing Songs or Hymns, they are to stand up with their Hands joyn'd together. 4. When Prayers are made for the Sanctification of the Sacrifices, then every one bends the left Knee, and stretches out his Arms wide open. But when the Victims are a slaying, every one may sit upon the ground (for they have no Seats or Pews, such as you use here in England) only the Richer sort have a Cushion to sit on; while the Flesh is a boyling, every one stands with his Hands joyn'd together, looking towards the upper Part of the Tabernacle. After the Flesh is boyl'd, every one of the People takes a piece of the Flesh from the Priest and eats it, and what remains, the Priests keep for themselves.

When all these Ceremonies are ended, the Tabernacle is opened, and then every one for sometime lies prostrate on the ground to adore; and after they rise up, they may look upon their God, and if he appears in the shape of an Ox, or such-like tame Beast, then they leap for Joy, because they believe that God is well-pleas'd with them: But if he appears in the shape of a Lyon, then they think some Great Crime has been committed, whereby God is much offended, and .

therefore they endeavour by New Sacrifices to appease him. After the Tabernacle is open'd and every one has ador'd, then there is a Sermon, and while that lasts, the People stand; and after Sermon, there is a short Prayer, and then a Thanksgiving; after which the people bow down their Body, and touch the ground with the fore-finger of their right Hand, and then depart.

When the Sun, Moon and Stars, are ador'd upon the Mountain, then they bend the right Knee, and hold up the right Hand toward Heaven; when that Chapter of Jarhabadiond is read, wherein our God commands them to Worship, the same posture of Body is observ'd in their Songs and Hymns, they stand with their Hands joyn'd together. In their Prayers they bend the left Knee and stretch out their Arms. At their Thanksgiving the People stand, looking towards Heaven with their Arms extended and wide open; and the same posture they use on their common Days, when they worship the Sun and the 5 Stars; but at Night when they worship the Moon and the 5 Stars, they stand with their Hands joyn'd together. And this is all that is remarkable, as to the several postures of Body they use in their Religious Worship.

CHAP. X

Of the Ceremonies that are observ'd at the Birth of Children

BY THE COMMAND of our God, the following Ceremonies are observ'd at the Birth of Children. 1st, When the Mother feels the time of Birth approaching, she ought to offer Sacrifices to the 10 Stars, more or less precious according to her Ability. After she is brought to Bed of a Child, she is to keep the Infant until the 1st Day of the Week, and on that Day she is to wash herself and the Infant, and go unto the Temple with her Husband, and to carry the Infant with her, and there to offer a Sacrifice to our God. Then Prayers are made for the Infant, and thanks are return'd for her safe delivery: Then the Mother and Father do solemnly promise, that they shall be ready to deliver up the Child, (if it be a Son and not the first born) to be Sacrific'd to the Honour of God, whensoever it shall be call'd for. Then a small fire being kindled of straw, the chief Sacrificator takes the Child, and makes it pass through the flame 12 times; after which there comes another Priest, and anoints the Child's skin with Oyl, least it should suffer any prejudice by the flame. All these things being ended, the Mother takes the Child, and the Priest having read the Thanksgiving, she returns Home with it; where it is usual upon such occasions, for the Father and Mother to make an Entertainment for their Kindred, Friends, and some of the priests.

When the Child arrives at 9 Years of Age, then the Child is to go on a Festival Day unto the Temple with his Father and Mother, and there to make a Vow unto God, that since he was pleas'd not to desire him for a Sacrifice, he will faithfully observe whatsoever is commanded him in Jarhadiond: And the Father and Mother do promise on their part, that they will do whatever lies in their Power for the Honour of our God. And then the Priest reads a prayer and Thanksgiving and they all return Home. The 1st Ceremony is call'd Abdalain, or the Purification: the 2d is call'd Blado, or the Vow.

But here it is to be Noted, that tho we use this Ceremony of Purification, yet we do it not upon the account of any Original Sin in the Infant, which we are altogether Ignorant of: And yet because our God has commanded this Purification to be us'd, some of them believe that it is for the Corruption of our Nature; and others that it is for the Sins of our Ancestors, and chiefly of our Father and Mother: For we think that God Created this World in time, and replenish'd it with Men; but we believe that God did not Create Mankind in the same Corrupt State in which it now is, but that Men by degrees Corrupted themselves, and that they do daily more and more degenerate from their Primitive State. as we find too plainly by experience. This is no Article of our Faith, but only the Opinion of some concerning the Creation of the World, and the State of the 1st Men Created by God: But our Scripture makes no mention of these things.

CHAP. XI
Of our Marriage, or Groutacho

SINCE OUR GOD requires the Hearts of so many young Boys to be offered up in Sacrifice, therefore lest the whole Race of Mankind should by degrees be extirpated, he has permitted the Men, at least those of the Laity, to keep more Wives than one: And so some of them have 3, 4, 5, 6, or more Wives, every one according to his Estate, whereby he is able to maintain a greater or lesser number; but if any one takes more Wives then his means will maintain, he is to be beheaded: And therefore to prevent this, before any one Marries a Wife, he is to be examin'd whether he has sufficient means to maintain her: Thus they may have many Wives, that they may beget many Children every Year; of whom some of the Sons are Sacrific'd, but the Daughters are all preserv'd for Matrimony, as will appear more fully hereafter.

In the mean time this is well worthy to be observ'd, that neither the Brother can Marry his Sister, nor the Brother's Son his own Brother's Daughter; all Marriage within these 2 degrees of Consanguinity (but not within the other degrees) being so absolutely forbidden, that the High Priest himself cannot dispense with it.

Whenever therefore a Man has a mind to take a Wife, whether he has one or more Wives before or no, he is first to agree with the Father and Mother for their good will, and then to get the consent of the Daughter. After this, before he is Married, he is to make known his design to the Sacrificator, who is to enquire whether he has sufficient means to maintain this Wife he intends to Marry; And if he has, then all the Friends and Relations are call'd together, and the Bridegroom and Bride come along with them to the Gate of the Temple, where they are met by a Priest, or the chief Sacrificator, who asks them, what they desire to have done; to which the Bridegroom and Bride answer, they desire to be joyn'd together in Matrimony, after which answer they are permitted to enter into the Temple. The reason why they are thus interrogated before their Admission is this, because no Man may enter into the Temple with any Woman but his Wife, except at the time when he is to be Married. Being thus introduc'd into the Temple in order to their Marriage, which is always to be Celebrated on a simple Festival-Day, viz. On the 2d Day of the Month, they are first to say their Prayers, and then to offer Sacrifice; after which the Husband promises to be faithful to his Wife, i.e. That he will know no other Woman besides those to whom he is joyn'd in Matrimony, that he will exercise no Tyranny over this Woman, nor do any thing to her contrary to the Law of Nature, of God, or of Man, &c. Likewise the Wife promises to be faithful to her Husband, that she will know no other Man besides him, that she will be obedient to him in all things, &c. Then they are both to swear before their God, the Sun, Moon and Stars, that they will faithfully keep this Promise, and to imprecate the Divine Vengeance if they shall break this solemn Vow. Then Prayers are said for them, after which they return Home with all their Company; at which time it is Customary to make a great Feast for them, according to the Estate of the Bridegroom. These things concern the Ceremony of Marrying, but as to other things relating to a Married State, they shall be mention'd in their proper Places.

CHAP. XII

Of the Ceremonies towards the Dead

THE SAME CEREMONIES are observ'd towards every one that is Dead, whether it be a Man or a Woman.

In the first place, many Prayers are put up and Sacrifices offer'd for the sick Person: But after Death, the Dead Body is to be kept 32 Hours, and to be anointed with Oyl, whether it be to be burnt by Day or by Night. After this, a little while before the Hour wherein it is to be burnt, all the Friends and Relations of the Deceas'd are sent for, and in their presence the Dead Body is plac'd in a Coffin, which Coffin is plac'd upon a Table: And then all the Company that had been invited, sit down at this Table which is furnish'd with all sorts of Meat, of which they eat freely. At last, when the Hour is come that the Body must be carried away to the place of Burial, then come the Priests both Regular and Secular, and the Players upon Musical Instruments, and the Mourners, i.e. those who Act the art of Mourners for Money; And all these being come, the Coffin is laid upon a Litter carried by 2 Elephants. All which may be better understood by the Figure here annex'd. But it is to be remark'd, that in the Description we have given of the Funeral Rites, we suppose the Person Deceas'd to die Rich; for as to others, the Poorer they are, the fewer Ceremonies are observed at their Funeral. Supposing therefore that the Person Deceas'd was Rich, after all the aforesaid Ceremonies are ended, which are to be observ'd at Home, then all the Company which ought to be present at the Funerals, meet together in the House of the Deceas'd, and having plac'd the Dead

Body in a Litter, they walk from the House to the place where the Body is burnt in this order: First, one of the Officers of the City leads the Van, carrying the banner of the Deceas'd, then follow several Players upon Instruments making a doleful noise: After them (if the Person Deceas'd be a Nobleman, but not else) follow the Souldiers who are to guard the Body, whereof some are Arm'd with Lances, some with Bows and Arrows, and others walk with naked Swords in their Hands: After them follow the Regulars, before whom goes the Officer of the Convent, carrying the Arms of God and of the Abby; after him follows the Monks, and last of all comes the Abbot. After them come the Secular Priests, and before them the Officer of the Parish Walks, carrying the Ensigns of God and of the Temple, there come all the common Priests, and after them the Sacrificator of the Sun, and then of the Moon and of the 10 Stars; after them come the Sacrificators of our God, and last of all the Chief Sacrificator with his Servants attending him: As to the High-Priest he never uses to be present at any Funeral, but when a King or a Vice-Roy are Dead; but after the Chief Sacrificator follow the Priests, and then come the Chariots full of Beasts for Sacrifice, which are carried by Elephants or Camels: After them come the Mourners who walk before the Dead Body, which is carried in a black Litter like those here in England, (saving that the middle is rais'd up to a point like the top of a Turret,) by 2 Elephants, the first whereof, that which goes before the Corps, is cover'd all over with black Cloth, so that nothing of it is to be seen but the Head; and on the Cloth, are fasten'd the Coats of Arms of all the Ancestors of the Deceased, as his Grand-Fathers, Great Grand-Fathers, and his Parents, all which are distinctly plac'd; And lastly, after the Litter, follow first the Parents and Kindred, and then the Friends of the Deceased, Now when all this Company is come to the place where the Dead Body is to be burnt, then the Priests Regular and Secular are to pray for the purification of the Sacrifices: After this the Beasts are slain and burnt, upon an Altar which is built there

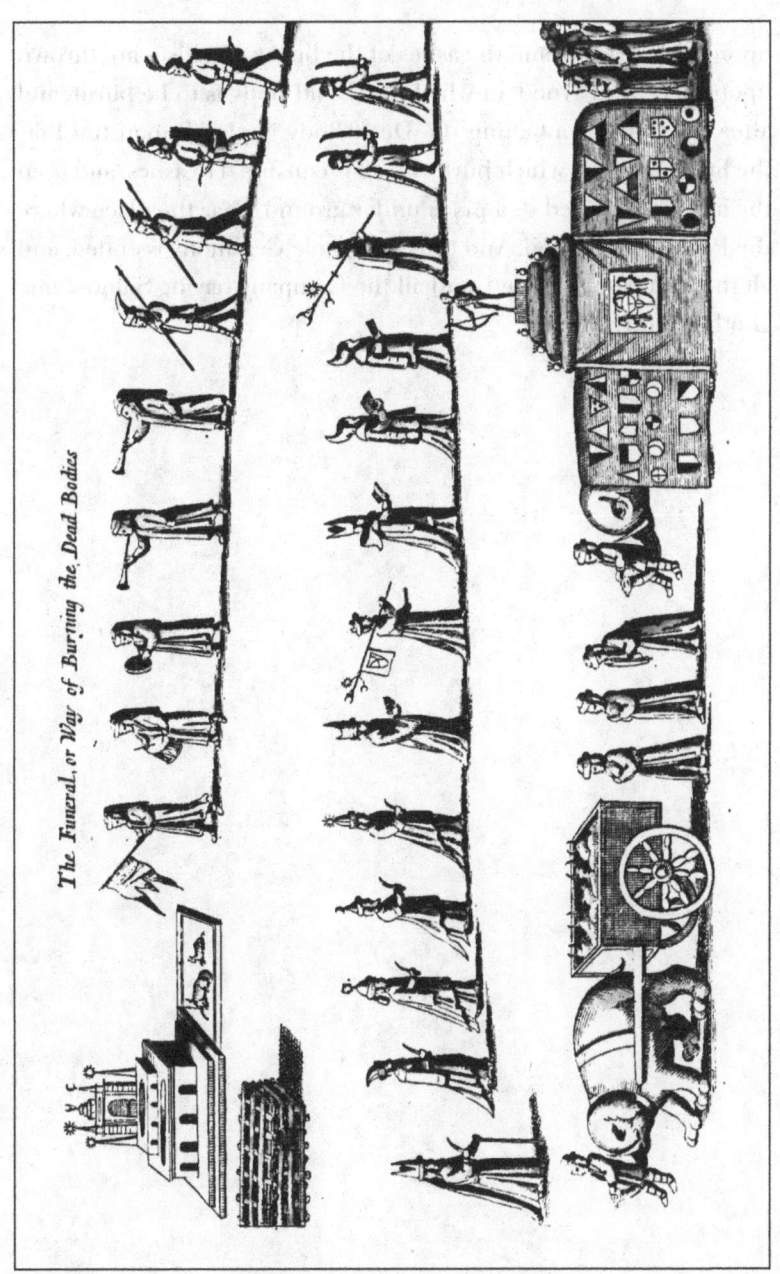

The Funeral, or Way of Burying the Dead Bodies

upon this occasion, and the ashes of the burnt Sacrifises are thrown upon the Pile of Wood, in which the Dead Body is to be burnt; and after the Coffin containing the Dead Body is plac'd upon the Pile, the fire is put to it, which burns till all is consum'd to ashes; and then the ashes are buried in a place under ground, near the place where the Pile of wood stood. And thus the whole Ceremony is ended, and all the Company is ended, and all the Company having Saluted one another return Home.

CHAP. XIII

Of our Opinion concerning the State of Souls after Death

SINCE OUR SCRIPTURE or the Book, which they call Jarhabadiond, promises great happiness after this Life, to those who have liv'd according to the Natural, Divine and Human Laws, but says nothing expressly of the State of Souls after Death, hence we are divided into various Opinions about it. The Transmigration of Souls is generally believ'd by all of them, which appears to have been the common and ancient Opinion of almost all Pagans; but as to the manner of this Transmigration we differ: For some believe that the Soul after Death, passes into the Body of some Beast, either wild or tame, some that it passes into the body of another Man, either Poor or Rich, Happy or Miserable, according to its behaviour in the former body good or bad, and so it continues to pass out of the body of one Beast into another, or of one Man into another, in endless circuits of happiness and misery. Others have more sublime Notions of a departed Soul, for they believe that the Soul which is to be rewarded with Happiness after this Life, shall at last be transform'd into a Star, and then being plac'd in Heaven, it shall enjoy all imaginable Happiness, which will consist in the vision and fruition of our God: But because the Sins of such a Soul design'd for this Happiness, which have been committed in this Life, are not always fully and perfectly blotted out before Death, but only cover'd, by the Sacrifices that have been offer'd for them; therefore they appoint a certain place, in which the Soul, before it arrives at this Happiness, may do penance for its Sins, which place they think to be the bodies of some

Beasts: And for this reason, they believe that God forbids the use of these Beasts for Food, and will not suffer them to be kill'd, but only for Sacrifices, viz. Oxen, Rams, Elephants, Harts, Goats, Doves, Dogs, Horses, Camels, &c. All which Beasts are forbidden to be slain by any one, but only for Sacrifices; and if any of them die of themselves, then they are Buried after their Death, least they should be devour'd by wild Beasts. They believe therefore, that these Souls design'd for Happiness, shall remain in the bodies of Beasts, until they have done penance for the Sins committed in their former bodies; But after such a Beast dies of it self, or is offer'd in Sacrifice to our God, then they believe that the Soul which was in it, shall be transformed into a Star in Heaven, where it shall enjoy eternal Happiness.

But all this seems to me to be a fiction invented by our Priests, because they reap great profit and advantage by it; for when any one dies, the Relations of the Deceased, are to pay them a great Sum of Money, more or less, according to their Ability, which they promise to convey to the Soul under penance: For they perswade the People, that the Souls under penance stand in need of Money, which none know how to transmit to them but themselves: And besides, they receive as much Money for the Prayers and Sacrifices, that are offer'd for these Souls while they continue in a State of penance.

As for the damn'd Souls, they determine nothing for a certain truth, but are divided into various Opinions. For some think that these Souls shall inform the Bodies of evil Beasts, as they call the Lyons, Wolfs, Tigers, Apes, Cats, Swine, Serpents, and other such like Beasts. Others believe that they are in a manner annihilated, after they depart out of the Body of a Man: But the more common Opinion is that of those, who believe that they wander eternally in the Air, and that God Creates in them such a pain for the loss of their Happiness, and such a shame for the Sins they have committed, as fills them with a grief too great for Human Nature to bear. And these damn'd Souls they believe to be, what here in Europe you call Devils, and there they call os Pagostos: And therefore they offer Sacrifices to these evil Spirits, because they believe that these Sacrifices give them some ease of their pain, and so hinder them from doing themselves a mischief.

CHAP. XIV

Of the Priestly Garments

THE PRIESTS WERE formerly left at their liberty to wear any kind of Garments they pleas'd, provided they were such as would distinguish them from the Laity: But now they have different kinds of Garments, every one according to their several Offices; which Custom is never any more to be alter'd. What these Garments are may appear by the following description of them, The High Priest has a Sky-colour'd Mitre, the lower part of which is shap'd like a Crown, and is plac'd upon a Bonnet; the Hair of his Head is short, and of his Beard long; he wears a little Cloak of a Sky-colour, which is round before, tapering behind, and reaches down only to the Elbow. He wears also a long Cloak like a Gown, which hath sleeves open in the middle thro' which he puts his Arms, and that also is of a Sky-colour. Under this Cloak there is a Cloth of a Violet-colour, which hangs down before and behind, and also a white Tunick. His stockins are such as are commonly worn, but he has no breeches. He wears shoes like Sandals, such as are commonly us'd by the Capuchirzes in the Romish Church. He carries an Iron-Rod in his Hand, being a Cubit long, having a round Head on which his Coat of Arms is Engraven.

The chief Sacrificator has also a Mitre upon his Bonnet, but no shape of a Crown, and from the round part of the Bonnet there hangs a Cloth which reaches down to the ground: He has also a Long Gown which is tied about with a Girdle. The Mitre is of a Sky-colour, signifying his dignity, and the Bonnet of a Red colour, signifying his Office of Sacrificator. The Cloth which hangs down from his Bonnet is of a Sky-colour, and his Gown is Red: He always carries a sword in his Hand, in token of his bloody Office; his Shoes and Stockens are like those of the High Priest, and his Girdle is usually of a White-colour.

The common Sacrificator of our God, has a sharp-Pointed Bonnet of a Red-colour, bending a little downward behind: He wears a Cloak like that of the High-Priest, but of a Red-colour, and it is so short before, that it coven only the Knee; and behind, it hangs down to the ground: He has also a Red Gown under his Cloak.

The Sacrificaton of the Sun, Moon and 10 Stars have the same Garments, but of a different colour. The Sacrificator of the Sun, has a white Bonnet with the figure of the Sun on the top of it: He wears also a red Cloak and a white Tunick. The Sacrificator of the Moon, has a white Bonnet, and the figure of the Moon for distinction upon the top of it, a white Coak and a red Gown. The Sacrificator of the 10 Stars has the figure of them upon a white Bonnet, and behind, there is a short piece of Cloth hanging down from the Bonnet, he wears a red Cloak with a white Sleeve, and a white Tunick. All Sacrificators carry a Sword in their Hand.

The common Priests have a kind of a Bonnet, upon which there is a short Mitre, shorter behind than before: They wear a long Gown of a white colour, whose Sleeves are long and broad; they do not tye their Gown with a Girdle, but they have a short Tunick under it made of Cotton.

The Officers or Servants belonging to the Temples, have also a habit distinct from the Laity, for they wear a Bonnet different from the common People, a black Gown, and a black Rod about a Cubit long; and at all the common Meetings they carry the Arms of the Parish, and of Religion like a Banner.

The Regular Priests wear the like Garments with the Secular, but they are of a different colour, according to their several Abbies. They have a sharp-pointed Cowie upon their Head; they shave the hair of their Head often, but never their Beard: They have a long Tunick, and over it a short one, but both of them are close: The sleeve of their upper Gown, which is short, but large, usually hangs down low. Their stockens and shoes are like those of other Priests. Their Superior at publick Meetings has a Mitre upon his Head, and his Cowie hangs down behind: Besides, he has a little short Cloak like that of the High-Priests, but it is of a Violet-colour; and a Violet-colour'd Cloth hanging down before and behind, and a long Tunick of a white-colour, and lastly a long Cloak between the Tunick and the little Cloak, which usually is of Divers Colours: He ought to have a long Beard and short Hair on his Head, he carries an iron-rod in his Hand like the High-Priest; his shoes and breeches are like the rest of the Regulars: But when he is in the Abby, he wears the same kind of Cloaths as the other Monks.

The Servants of the Abby are Cloth'd after the same manner, as the Servants of the Temple, except as to the Bonnet, which is such a Bonnet as the Boys wear here in London; their other Garments are distinguish'd only by their Colours. And this is all that occurs to me at present, as to their Habits and Religion.

All which habits may be seen in the Figure of their Funerals, where all these habits of the Priests are exactly represented.

CHAP. XV

Concerning their Manners and Customs

'TIS CERTAIN THAT the Manners of the Formosans, are not so Corrupt as the People are in other Places; and the reason is, because they are strictly oblig'd to observe the Laws of their Policy and Religion under severe Penalties, with which the Laws are enforc'd against the Commission of any Villany or Impiety; so that none dare to violate them, being restrain'd by the dread of their Penalties, which are certainly and impartially Executed.

They have divers Customs which will please some, and displease others: For first, 'tis customary with them to adore the Emperor as a God: He never sets his Foot upon the ground, nor suffers the Sun to shine upon his Face. None but Noblemen are permitted to Visit him, nor are the Inferior People admitted to see him, except at the Great Festivals, which are but 3 in a Year; and then he shows himself to all the People: But first, they are to bend their Knees and fall prostrate on the ground, and adore him: After they have done this, they may rise up and look upon him.

They Salute the Kings by bending their Knee, joyning their Hands and bowing their Head. They Salute the Vice-Roys also by bending one Knee, (viz. The Left, if he be the Vice-Roy of a Foreign King, and the Right if he be Vice-Roy of one of his own Kings) and also by carrying his Right Hand from his Head down to the ground.

They Salute an High-Priest as they do a King, and the chief Sacrificators as they do Vice-Roys. The Noblemen and Priests are Saluted by carrying the Hand from the Head down to the shoe, and by bowing the Head. One Friend Salutes another by kissing both his Hands, and joyning them with his Friends, Superiors do not Salute an Inferior, but by a nod of their Head they signify, that they have seen him Saluting them. Servants Salute their Masters, by carrying their Hand from their Mouth down to the ground, and falling prostrate on their Face. Wives do Salute, and are Saluted after the same manner as their Husbands. In speaking to Noblemen, they use not any particular distinct Language as the Chinese do, nor any Circum-locutions, or different way of Construction from what is us'd to Inferior Persons, but calling them by their Title; and in speaking to them, and even to the Emperor himself, they make use of the second Person of the singular Number: And this is the Customary way of speaking to Great Men, which is observ'd in all Japan.

No Conversation is allow'd between any Man and another Man's Wife, nor between a Batchelor and a Maid, but in the greatest Feasts and Diversions, every one keeps among those of their own Family, the Wives with their own Husband, the Sons. and Daughters with their Father and Mother; for if any Man should see one Man with another's Wife, or a Maid with a Batchelor that is a stranger, he would certainly account them Adulterers.

Supposing that a Man has 6 Wives, each Wife has a private Chamber for her self, in which she lives with her own Sons and Daughters, and takes pains in some kind of work, and when the hour of Dinner or Supper comes, a Servant goes and knocks at their Doors; and then they come our of their Chambers into the Parlour where they are to eat. After Dinner, they may walk for sometime with their Husband in the Garden, and then every one of them returns to her own Chamber again, and continues there until the time of Supper; only sometimes they are allow'd to meet, and drink together, such Liquors as Thea, Chila, &c. As soon as the hour of Supper is come, then a Servant goes and calls them all, and they come to Supper. After Supper they walk, and divert themselves with

Dancing, Singing, or telling old stories, or any such like Recreation. At last, at the third hour of the Night (which is the 9th hour here in England) every one of them goes to her own Chamber, and the Husband sends for one of them whom he has a mind to lye with that Night; and in the Day-time he sometimes Visits one of them, sometimes another, according to his fancy. This kind of Life is sweet and pleasant enough, as long as every one of them is of an agreeable humour; but if the Husband begins to love one Wife more then another, then arises Envy and Emulation against that Woman whom he loves most, and hence strife and discord is spread thro' the whole Family: But when the Husband is civil and discreet, and imparts to each of them an equal share of his good will and friendship, then all the Wives endeavour to please him in all things, and the House is like a Paradise, by their good agreement, and dutiful care of their Husband. The Women employ themselves in some kind of work proper for them, in teaching and taking care of their Children: And sometimes they Visit one another, or spend their time in Innocent Recreations. And while they continue dutiful and peaceable, they may have any thing of their Husbands that they desire: Who always Marry them when they are very young, viz: Between 10 and 15 Years of Age, that they may the more easily bend them to comply with their humor. Every Wife takes care of her own children; but if one die and leave Children behind her, then the Husband Marries another and commits the care of them to her.

This Prerogative is granted to the first Wife above all the rest: That she is to take care of the Family, and is not so much subject to the Husband as the others are; for the other Wives cannot go out of the House, unless the Husband be with them, but the first Wife may. Besides, her first Son is never to be Sacrific'd, but is the Heir of the Family, as we shall show hereafter; and when the Husband dies, the first Wife governs the Family, and the rest are subject to her. And this Custom prevails also among the Japanners, but with this difference:

That the Japan Women after the Death of their Husband may Marry again, but the Formosan cannot; the former receives some Portion of their Father's Estate, but the latter do not.

When any Man has a mind to Marry a Maid, with whom he is in love, he must first acquaint the Father and Mother with his design, and discover to them what Estate he has, &c. And if the Father and Mother consent to give him their Daughter in Marriage, then he is permitted to speak to the Daughter, but never before: Neither then is he allow'd to converse with her in private, but only in the presence of the Father or Mother, or one of the Maids Kindred: And if the Daughter consent, then the Father and Mother present him with some Gift of small Value, as a Ring, some Clothes, or the like, but they give him no Portion out of the Father's Estate with her.

The first Born Son of the first Wife, as has been already noted, is not to be Sacrific'd, and is the Heir of the Family: Now the Right of Inheritance consists in this, that he receives one half of the Estate after the Father's Death: But the Brethren divide the other half among them; and if every one of them will Marry a Wife before the Death of the Father, then the Wife whom he Marries, continues in the Husband's Family until the Father be Dead, and then the Estate is divided, and each Brother takes his share of it, and lives by himself.

'Tis Customary on Solemn Days, between the first and last day of a Festival, for all sorts of People, to Feast their Relations and Friends, as they use to do at Births, Marriages and Burials, which has been already observ'd.

The Poor are not suffer'd to beg in the Isle Formosa, but every Precinct has some Puhlick House, wherein they keep all their Poor, who are Fed and Cloth'd at the Charge of the whole Precinct; and those of them who are able, are put to Work and Labour, but others who are disabled by Age or Sickness, are maintain'd Gratis, This Publick House is call'd the House of God for the Poor, or in the Language of the Natives, *Caa tuen pagot ack chabis-collinos*. If any stranger, who comes from some other Island of the Japan Empire, happens to want subsistence while he is Travelling thro' the Country, he is furnish'd with Necessaries in every City and Village that he passes thro' at the expence of the publick.

They have also Taverns and VictuallingHouses, which Men frequent for Eating and Drinking, Smoking and Playing, &c. But no Woman must come into any of these Publick Houses.

All Japanners were wont to be very curious to see strangers, and to entertain them very civilly; but ever since the great slaughter was made of the Christians that were there, they hate all strangers that come into their Country, unless they come from some other Island of Japan, as will appear more fully hereafter.

CHAP. XVI

A Description of the Men in Formosa

ALTHO' THE COUNTRY be very hot, yet the Men in all Formosa are very fair, at least those who can live upon their Means; but the Country People, Servants, and others, who are expos'd to the heat of the Sun, and are forc'd to work in the open Air all Day, are very much tawn'd by the burning heat. The Men of Estates, but especially the Women, are very fair; for they during the hot season, live under ground in places that are very cold; They have also Gardens and Groves in them so thick set with Trees, that the Sun cannot penetrate thro' them; and they have Tents which they use to sprinkle with water, so that the heat can do them no hurt: And hence it comes to pass, that altho the Formosans live in a hotter Country than the English, yet they cannot so well endure heat.

They use Distill'd Waters, not only to wash themselves, but also to remove any speck upon the skin, which is not rooted in the flesh: And this is one means which makes them so fair.

And here I must not omit to give some account of a Controversie, between the Chinese and Japannese on the one side, and the Natives of Formosa on the other, relating to the Customs of these Countries. Ye must know then that the Chinese and Japannese make their Teeth artificially black, but the Formosans preserve them white. The Jappanese plead for their Custom, that all Beauty consists in Variety of Colours, and therefore as an Ethiopian is counted most Beautiful, who has a black Face and white Teeth; So the Beauty of the Natives in our Country who have a fair Face, must consist in having black

Teeth. But the Formosans granting this argument, answer for themselves, that Beauty may consist in some things, which cannot be had: Thus it would be Beautiful to have black Eyes, which yet cannot be made so, and therefore, say they, nothing artificial ought to be made use of, to make us appear otherwise than Nature has fram'd us.

Hence the Reader may observe, that the Formosans are also white and very fair, but chiefly the Women; and if we may believe the Proverb, Turkey and Japan breeds the fairest Women in the World. The Formosans, generally speaking, are of a short stature, but they make up in thickness what they want in tallness. They are commonly strong-bodied Men and indefatigable in Labour; they are very good Souldiers, and love War better then Peace. They are very kind and good-natur'd towards their Countrymen: Whom they love, they love so well, that they would lose their Lives for them in a case of necessity; but whom they hate, they hate mortally, and usually contrive their Death in any way that's possible to them. They are very Industrious and Cunning, and quickly learn any thing they see done before them. They abhor all falsehood and lying, and therefore they have no value for Tradesmen and Shopkeepers, because they use many lies to commend their Wares, and put them off at a better Price.

CHAP. XVII

Of the Cloaths worn in Formosa, by all Ranks of People

THE FORMOSANS ARE certainly very curious in their Cloaths, but they affect no new fashion as the Europians do; wherefore they seem to be still Cloathed according to their Ancient Custom. In this they excel the Europeans, that the Qualities and Conditions of Men may be discern'd there by the distinction of their Habits, whereas here a Nobleman cannot be known from a Tradesman by his Cloaths. The Habits of the Formosans are not much different from those of the Jappannese, especially as to the common sort of People; but the Kings and Vice-Roys, and Noblemen have different sorts of Garbs. The great difference between the Jappannese and Formosan, consists in this, that the Jappannese wear 2 or 3 Coats, which they tye about with a Girdle; but the Formosans have only one Coat, and use no Girdle. They walk with their Breast open, and cover their Privy pans with a Plate tied about them made of Brass, Gold, or Silver. The Jappannese also wear little light Bonnets, but the Formosans use larger Bonnets, with a train hanging down to the ground, made of some light stuff, as Silk. Cotton, &c. And when they walk. they wrap it about their Arm.

We shall add no more about the Jappannese, since our design is only to give an account of the Isle Formosa: And seeing, as I have said, the dignity and condition of every one may be discern'd by their different Habits, I shall now briefly describe them.

The King wears a short Coat of Silk, which he ties with a most precious Girdle, and above that a long open Gown made of very costly Silk, wrought with Gold and Silver: He has a scarf that hangs

The King

over the Right Shoulder, and reaches down to the left side, of Cloth of Gold or Silver curiously wrought with the Needle, which is the Badge of his Dignity. He wears also a Bonnet, from whose top the stuff hangs down to the ground, which Bonnet is encompass'd with a kind of a Crown, that glisters with precious Stones and Carbuncles. He has no Breeches, but his Knees are naked; he wears stockens made of Silk, adorn'd with many Ribbons. His shoes, like those of the Priests afore-mention'd, are a sort of Sandals, but most curiously wrought. When he or any Nobleman Rides, then he wears Stockens and Breeches together in one piece, and a little Bonnet. His Collar is made of Silk, but set with precious Stones; the Hair of his Head is short, as is usual thro' all Japan, and his Beard is about a Thumb's length.

The Queen wears most Beautiful Garments, that glister with precious Stones; she has no such Headgear as the Women wear here in England, but something made of Gold or Silver wrought with Silk, and so adorn'd with Diamonds, that it seems to be a Crown. Her Neck-cloth is made of some precious matter: Her Garments are very precious, curiously wrought with the Needle and long enough to reach down to her Heel; and the upper part of her sleeve is so broad that it touches the ground, as does also her Manto which hangs down so low behind. Her shoes and stockens are like her Husband's, but of a less size, and have a higher Heel. She wears her Hair hanging down behind, over her Gown which is not wide, nor hath many plaits. She wears a Girdle tied about her body very precious.

The Sons are clad after the same manner as the Father; only instead of the short Gown, they go with their Breasts wide open, and have a half-girdle about their Loyns. They wear not a Bonnet until they be 9 Years old. The Daughters also are Cloath'd after the same manner as the Mother, except as to their Headgear, for they wear nothing upon their Head, but a little Crown made of Bowers, or the feathers of some Bird; and they have no Manto.

The Queen

The Viceroy

The Vice-Roy who had formerly been a King, is still very splendid in his Cloaths. His Bonnet is very great and precious, both for the matter of it, and the Curiosity of the Workmanship, and it is adorn'd with precious Stones; the Hair of his Head, and his Beard is short; his Collar is of black Silk finely wrought with Silver. He wears a short Coat of white Silk, which is tied about with a precious Girdle, and over that a long Gown open and wide; he has also a Scarf like the King, which hangs on the right-shoulder down to the left-side; and lastly, over his shoulders he has a little Cloak made of red and black Silk; his Vest is lin'd with the skin of some Tyger or Leopard; he has no breeches, but only stockens, and his shoes are like those afore-mention'd.

The Vice-Roys Queen is Dress'd much after the same manner as the Queen, saving that the Queen has a Coyff, such as above-describ'd; but the Vice-Roy's Queen, wears only her own Hair adorn'd with Silk and Ribbons: Her Gown is made after the same fashion as the Queen's; but her Manto is different in this, that the Queen's Manto hangs down behind only from her shoulders; but that of the Vice-Roy's Queen is like a large Morning-Gown, which is worn here in England: Only it wants sleeves, and is lin'd with some Beautiful skin. The Vice-Roy's Son has 2 Coats, a short one and another long; but the shorter one is uppermost, and comes down only to the Knee: His Daughters are clad after the same manner as the Mother, saving that they have no Manto.

The Noblemen wear the same Coats as the Vice-Roy, but with this difference, that the Vice-Roy has no Girdle about his long Coat, which the Noblemen have: They wear a Scarf of Silk from the right-shoulder to the left-side but their Bonnet is like that of the Citizens.

The Carillan, or Chief-General, has a Bonnet like the Vice-Roys, but not so Great: In the fore-part it is adorn'd with a Diamond and Precious Stones: His Collar is of Silk, which encompasses his Neck, but does not hang down. Instead of a Scarf, he has a short

The Vicercy's Lady

Cloak of Silk, which covers only his shoulders; and a short Tunick of Silk; his breeches and stockens are tied together; his shoes are like other Men's: And lastly, he has a long and wide open Gown, like the Morning Gowns that are worn here, but much larger, whose sleeves being open in the middle, he puts his Arms through, and the rest of the sleeves hang low down towards the Ground. His Wife is clad like the Vice-Roy's Queen, saving that she does not wear a Manto; His Sons and Daughters, are Cloath'd after the same manner as the Vice-Roy's.

The Wives of Noblemen, wear a little Bonnet made of artificial Bowers: They have 2 Tunicks, one that's long, and a short one over that which comes down only to the Knee, which they tie about with a Girdle, There is an Handkerchief fasten'd to their Bonnet, which hangs down to their shoulders. Their Sons and Daughters are Cloath'd after the same manner as those of the Carillan.

The Citizens wear one Gown only, ought to keep the Hair of their Head short, have a Bonnet like the Noblemen, whose top made of Silk or Cotton, reaches down to the ground: They wear a Collar, but no shirt, except in the Night-time when they go to Bed, which is the Custom of them all. They walk in a long Gown with Naked Breast and Thighs, but their Privy parts are cover'd with a Plate tied about them made of Brass or Silver, or Gold: Their stockens and shoes are such as are commonly us'd by others.

Their Sons have a little Bonnet, a short Gown tied about with a Girdle, which reaches down to the middle of their Thigh: They have shoes like their Father, but neither breeches nor stockens.

The Country People who dwell in Villages and Desert-places, wear nothing but a Bears skin upon their shoulders, and a Plate to cover their Privy-parts made of Brass or the shells of Fish, or the bark of Trees, Their Sons have nothing but a Scarf hanging on their right shoulder down to their left side, but otherwise they are stark Naked. When the Countrymen are Rich, they and their Sons wear a

Girdle about their Loyns, which half covers their Thighs instead of a Plate tied with a Girdle to cover their Privy-parts.

The Female Sex is distinguish'd also among the common sort of People by 5 kinds of Habits. Infants, Virgins, Brides, Married Women and Widows, all of which are clad in different Apparel. Infants wear a short Gown that reaches down to the middle of their Thigh; they have stockens and shoes like others, but they do not cover their Head until they be 9 Years old. Virgins after they are 9 Years old, adorn their Head with Birds feathers, or artificial flowers done up with Ribbons: They wear a short Gown above another, that is long and reaches to the ground, both which they tie about them with a green Girdle. The long Gown is divided into two in the lower part, so that their Legs appear as high as their Knee. They have stockens and shoes like other Women.

The Brides at the time of their Marriage do wonderfully adorn themselves; their Head is encompass'd round with Flowers, Laurels and Feathers, which make a great show: They have two Coats equally long, whereof the under Coat is white and the upper black, and both of them are tied with a black Girdle. They wear a Scarf of red Silk hanging on the left shoulder down to the right side. The black Gown which is uppermost is open, so that the white Petticoat underneath may be seen. And after this manner they are clad during all the time of Courtship, but 9 Days after the Celebration of Marriage, they put on the Habit of Married Women.

The Married Women wear a long open Gown, and below it a short Coat which reaches down to their Knee. They have a kind of a Cap upon their Head like a Platter, and let their Hair hang down in wreaths before their Breast; and when they go out, they so cover their Face, that it can hardly be seen.

Widdows have another kind of a Cap which is twofold: The first which they put on their Head, is almost round like an English Woman's Coyff, the other is a little sharp-pointed. They dress their

Hair in wreaths; they wear 2 Gowns, one long and another short one over it; the short one ought always to be of a black colour, but the other, which may be of any other colour, has long and broad sleeves, which reach down to the Knee; and both the Gowns are tied about with a Girdle.

The Country Women have nothing but a Bear's skin upon their shoulders, and a Cloth about their middle which reaches down to their Knee: They tye a piece of Linnen about their Head and Hair; they have no stockens, but shoes, such as are worn by others. Their Daughters wear nothing but a Cloth about their middle, and a Scarf on the right shoulder hanging down to the· left side, and they have shoes like their Mother.

And here 'tis to be observ'd, that all of them generally wear a Bracelet about their Arm; but the Women wear it both about their Arm and their Neck. And this is all that I know to be remarkable as to their Apparel; I shall now only add something as to the Military Habit.

The King of the Isle Formosa has his own Guards, and so has the Vice-Roy, and therefore for distinction-sake they are differently clad. All the Officers in the King's Guards are clad like the Carillan, saving that the Carillan wears a Carbuncle upon his Bonnet which they have not, and they wear a Scarf which he has not.

The King's Guards have a round Bonnet, whose forepart is like a Mitre, and has the King's Arms upon it: The Hair of their Head is short, and of their Beard long; and they have also a Breast-plate or Stomacher made of Silver on which are the King's Arms; a Belt made of Silk, a short Gown, and stockens and breeches in a piece: They wear a Sword hanging by their left side, and the Weapons they use when they Guard the King, are the Halberd or Lance.

The Officers of the Vice-Roys Guards are Cloathed like the Tana's or Noblemen, saving that they have not a Scarf, and use a short Bonnet like the King's Guards. All the several Degrees of Officers

are distinguish'd by Colours, at the pleasure of the King or Vice-Roy.

The Guards of the Vice-Roy wear a large long Bonnet having 2 Wings, a long Gown which they take up behind when they walk, breeches and stockens in a piece, the common sort of shoes: The Hair of their Head and Beard is short, and their Arms are short Lances, Arrows, and a Sword by their side.

All the Souldiers which serve to Guard the Cities are Cloath'd after the same manner, viz. They have a short Bonnet with a Crest of 2 or 3 feathers, a short Gown, stockens and breeches in a piece. All of them wear black Cloaths: Some are Archers and carry a Bow under their Arm, and have a Quiver full of Arrows; others are Spearmen, and carry a long Spear upon their shoulders; but others have short Spears.

The Drummers have a Bonnet sharp-pointed at top, with a piece of Brass in the Frontispiece of it, whereon are Engraven the Arms of the Isle. They wear a short Gown and a long one underneath it, which they throw behind them: Their Cloaths are of a light red colour.

The Ensigns have a Bonnet like the Noblemen, and they are all such who are in this Post. They wear a long Gown and a short one over it.

This is all that I thought worthy to be remark'd as to their Apparel, which altho it may appear ridiculous to the Europeans, yet is there accounted very Beautiful and Splendid, both for the Colours and the materials of which it is made, such as Hair, Silk, Cotton, which are curiously wrought with the Needle; for tho they do not affect new fashions of Cloaths, yet they are very nice in choosing the finest Stuff, or Cloth whereof to make them.

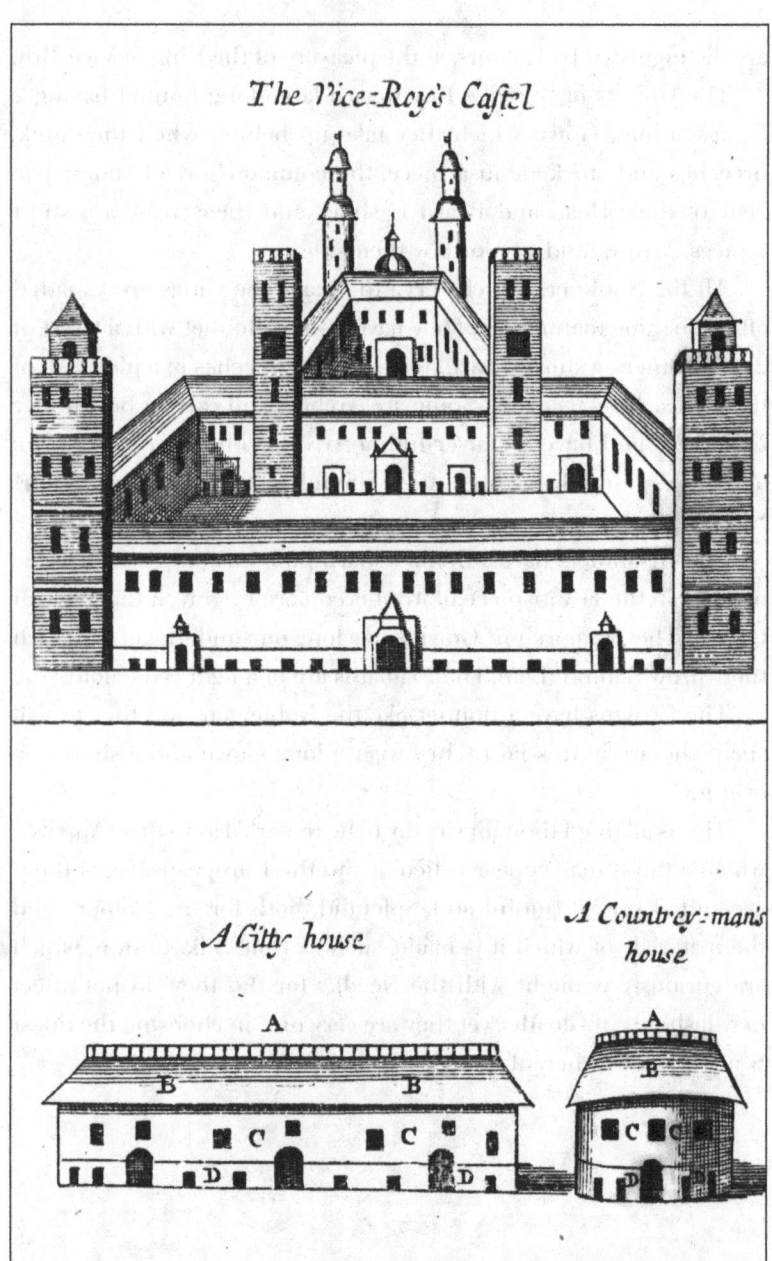

The Vice-Roy's Castel

A Citty house

A Countrey-man's house

CHAP. XVIII

Of their Cities, Houses, Palaces, Castles

THERE ARE ONLY SIX Towns in the Isle Formosa, which deserve the Name of a City: Two of them are in the Principal Island, and they are call'd Xternetsa and Bigno; there is one in great Peorko, which is call'd Chabat; and the 4th is in one of the Isles of Robbers and is call'd Arriow: The 5th and 6th are in the other Isle of Robbers, and they are call'd Pineto and Jarabut: But in the little Isle Peorko there are none, as will appear afterwards.

Xternetsa, as it is the Capital City, so it is the most Beautiful of all the rest; being situated in a very pleasant Plain: It's Walls are 20 Cubits high and 8 broad; It's length is about 1 Day's Journey for an Elephant, i.e. about sixteen English Miles. There are in it Desert-places, Fields and Mountains, Orchards, Meadows, and the like places which are not Inhabited; but about the middle of it, the Houses are very magnificent and stately: Not far from it, there is a Mountain which abounds with many whole som Springs. It is built by the side of a River, which was made there on purpose for its convenience; It abounds with Fish and runs over the whole Isle. That which contributes much to make it Beautiful, are the many Palaces that are in it, viz. Of the King, the Vice-Roy, and the Nobles; of the High-Priest and Chief Sacrificator; all which are built after a wonderful manner, as may appear by the Figure here annex'd, which is a Representation of the Vice-Roy's Palace.

This Palace is built of four-square stones, curiously cut, as all the rest are, whereof the greatest part is cover'd with Gold: This House alone is three English Miles in Circumference, having a great Ditch round about it. Besides there belong to it, Greens, Gardens, Walks, Groves, all which are enclos'd with a Wall.

The High-Priest and Vice-Roy have Palaces there almost as good; but the King and Carillan, whose Offices do not descend by Succession to their Posterity, do not care to have such stately Houses. But the Nobles have there very Beautiful and Magnificent Houses. There are also in the City Xternetsa 3 great Abbies, and 5 Temples, and many Beautiful Houses of the Citizens. 'Tis observable, that in the whole Isle Formosa there are no Houses very high, but in most Great Houses there are 2 stories, one above ground for the Cold season, and the other under ground for the Hot season; which in all respects are very Magnificent, whether you look upon them within or without.

The Rich Men and Nobles, build their Houses of four-square Stones; but others build the outer-part of plain Timber, while the inner-part is adorn'd with Painted Wood, or fine Earthen Ware Gilded and Painted, which the Natives there call Porchellano, but the English ChinaWare. The Citizens Houses are long, and the Country People's round, in such manner as they appear in the Figures here annex'd.

A. The Place above the Roof of the House, where they adore the Sun, Moon and Stars twice a Day. B. The Roof of the House. C. The Place above ground. D. The Place of the House which is under ground.

Nevertheless, such long Houses are sometimes to be found in the Villages, and those that are round in the Cities, at least in the remote Places of them.

Bigno is a fine City, but has nothing peculiar that is remarkable. In the same Principal, Island, is the Sea-Port Town call'd Kadzey, which is very large and contains many Villages, and yet because it is not Wall'd about, it is accounted only a Village.

Chabat, Arriow and Pineto are Cities, which have nothing peculiar that is remarkable, but in jarabut 'tis worth observation, that the City is build round about a Mountain, which is a Mile high; And upon the top of it, is built the Palace of the Governour, who from his House can see the whole City, and so can every Citizen from the Roof of his House behold the Governour's Palace. Besides in the same City, there is a Fountain representing an Elephant Dancing upon 2 Feet, which is 20 Cubits high, and throws forth water out of all the Parts of the Body.

This Fountain is believ'd by the Jappannese to have been built above 11500 Years ago, by a certain God or Hero, who had been Banish'd thither when the Isle was yet uninhabited. This God was call'd Arbalo, or Wanderer: And the story says, that when he had built this Fountain there, it furnish'd him with Fruit, flesh and sweet Wine; but that after such time as he left the Island, it became barren, and produc'd none of these things. After this Island came to be Inhabited, some Men coming there and finding the curious fabrick of this Fountain, convey'd water into it by Aquaeducts, from a Mountain which is in the midst of the City: From whence the Jappannese have still in their Temple Amida, the God Arbalo with a Painted Fountain. But the Natives of the Isle Formosa give no credit to this story: Tho they know not by whom, nor when this Fountain was built, yet they call the Place of the Fountain by the Name Arbalo.

The History I do not deliver for a certain Truth, but neither do I account it altogether fabulous; for it seems to me very probable that there is something of truth in it, and therefore for the explication of it, I shall add the following remarks.

And first, the Reader is to take notice, that all the Gods which are call'd by any particular Name, such as Amida, Xakha, Nakon, Arbalo, &c. Are only Saints, or Heroes and Illustrious Men, who in former times were deified, either for their reputed Sanctity or some Noble Exploits, or wonderful Feats which they had perform'd. Such an one was Arbalo, who is the God of Harvest among the Japanese, and whose Image is commonly set in the husk of a Grain of Barley. He is called Arbalo, i.e. a Wanderer, because he continually went about the Fields and Woods, blessing the Fruits of the Ground.

Now 'tis possible, that this Man while he was alive did something that displeas'd the Emperor, or the Dairo, for which reason he was Banish'd from his Native Country, and there is no difficulty in conceiving this: But how he should Travel from Japan to Formosa, which is 200 Leagues distant from it, and was then unknown to the Japanese, and uninhabited, is something difficult to apprehend. Let us therefore suppose, that this God Arbalo was descended of some Noble Race, for such are all the Heroes in Japan, who were either come of some Illustrious Family, or had been promoted to some Eminent Post of Honour: And this is the more probable, because if he had been some inferior and mean Family, he would rather have been punish'd with Death, than sent into Banishment for his offence. This being granted, we may suppose further, that this Honourable Person carried along with him as his Retinue a great Multitude of Servants, and was sent at first, to an Isle next adjoyning to Japan, and from thence passing on in a direct Line through many little Isles, (which are so near, that you may see from one to the other in a clear Day) he came at last in sight of Formosa, where out of Curiosity he Landed with his Servants; and finding it a pleasant and fruitful Country, he settled there for some time, and built the Fountain above-mention'd. And then we may suppose, that he return'd again to Japan, and sent from thence some Colonies to Inhabit Farmosa. But I must confess, that we have no History in Formosa, so Ancient as this, which is only to be found in Japan, and therefore we can give no account of any thing that happen'd between us and the Japonese, after this first Settlement; for we have lost all the Memoirs of our first Original, and the transactions which happen'd after the first Plantation of our Country, until the Japonese ravish'd our Kingdom from us, and restor'd it to the Empire of Japan. However it may appear from what has been said, that the story of Arbalo is not fabulous, nor so improbable as at first blush it may seem to be.

Besides these Cities already Nam'd, there are 3 Sea-Port Towns which exceed some Cities for bigness; but because they are not Wall'd about, they are held only Villages or Towns. These 3 are call'd Aok, Louctau, and Voo, and besides them, there are many other Villages of the like bigness. But this is to be noted of Villages, Sea Port Towns and others, that they all depend on their own Cities, and that the other Cities depend upon the Capital City Xternetsa.

In the little Peorko, there is neither City nor Village to be found: But concerning this Island it is to be observ'd, that at first it belong'd to the King who is now Vice-Roy, but afterwards the Priests purchas'd it, to feed in it the fourfooted Beasts which are design'd for Sacrifice: And now every one is oblig'd to give not the first Fruits of their flocks, but one out of every three Beasts that fall, which is to be kept there until it be fit to be Sacrific'd: And therefore in little Peorlo, there are only some Shepherd's who look after the Beasts that are fed in that Island, which is very fruitful in Grass and Hay, and might perhaps produce many other things if they were Planted there: But this is not done because it is design'd only for the Beasts aforesaid.

These are all the notable things that occur to me concerning their Cities, Villages and Houses; yet it must be acknowledg'd that there is a great deal of difference between the Cities of Formosa, and those of Japan, both for their Bigness and the Richness of their Materials, tho the Jappannese when they come to Formosa, cannot sufficiently admire its Cities, for their Beauty, Situation and Conveniences.

CHAP. XIX

Of the Commodities which they have, and some that they want

THE GREAT QUANTITY of Gold and Silver that is in Formosa, is that which brings them the greatest Profit; for in the Principal Island, they have two Mines of Gold and two of Copper, tho none of Silver; in Great Peorko there are 2 Mines, one of Gold and another of Silver. In one of the Isles of Robbers there is a Mine call'd a Gold-Mine, which is not valued in others Counties because it is not truly and properly Gold; but it is highly esteem'd in the Isle where it is found, because it is fitter for many necessary uses among them than Gold itself is. In the other Isle of Robbers there are 2 little Silver Mines; So that in all, there are 3 Mines of Gold and 3 of Silver. All these Mines formerly pertain'd to the Vice-Roy, but now the King has one third Part, and the Emperor another. Silver in Formosa is almost esteem'd as much as Gold, because it is fitter for use, being a softer Mettal which is more easily wrought into any shape. They have no Iron or Steel, but what the Jappannese bring thither, who have one Mine of Iron: And therefore Iron, and also Brass, which is brought from other Parts, is more esteem'd there than Gold and Silver: But Copper is very common among them.

Utensils and Dishes, are usually made of Gold or China Earth. Their Temples and Houses are often cover'd with Gold, both in Cities and Villages: But since the Hollanders came there and exchanged their Iron for our Gold, the Natives have more rarely made any Gold.

Lead and Tinn are not the product of the Isle, but they are

abundantly supplied with it from the Neighbouring Countries.

Silks, and Cotton, of two sorts, they have in great quantities, which are very Artificially Interwoven with God and Silver: One sort of Cotten grows upon Trees in bags and is of the green finer sort, another grows upon a Shrub like a Thistle and is a coarser sort. And this is the great Employment of the Women, who of these Materials make Clothes, Carpets, Tapestry, and such kind of things; wonderfully fine. Of Silk and Hair are made Velvet and Plush: But this kind of Work belongs to the Men and not to the Women. They have not Woollen-cloth because they know not how to make it, but they receive great quantities of this Cloth from the Hollanders. They make Stuffs of Hair and Cotton, but no Cloth of Flax, which does not grow there; but Flaxen Cloth they receive from the Dutch. They Work, paint, and Gild China-Earth very Wonderfully, nay even much finer then they do in China. They have learn'd from the Hollanders to make a kind of Paper, which they knew not how to do before; for they wrote either upon plates of Copper or upon Parchment. But now they Write on Paper made of Silk after the same manner as it is made here.

Instead of Leather to make Shoes of, they use the bark of Trees for the Soles, and some skins of Beasts to serve for the Upper-leather.

CHAP. XX

Of Weights and Measures

BEFORE THE DUTCH arriv'd on our Coasts, we had a certain way of reckoning things, whereby we could know when their Numbers were equal or unequal; but we had no kind of weight, such as a Pound or an Ounce, and therefore we bought and sold things by View, and not by Weight. But after the Hollanders came among us, and show'd us how Profitable the use of Pounds and Ounces would he in Commerce, we begun to weigh things that are rare by Ounces, and Pounds; but things that are common and less valuable, by 50, or 100/. weight at a time, as the Buyer and Seller had a mind. Our Pound agrees with the Dutch Pound, which consists of 16 Ounces, and is more then that Pound which is us'd in France: Which I found by a Copan of our Money that I brought with me to France, which weigh'd more then one of the French Pounds, tho it was but a Dutch Pound.

Things are measur'd in Formosa, according to the People's various humors, for some use a greater, some a less measure; but the price is always fix'd according to the Greatness of the measure.

The Instrument wherewith they weigh things, is such as is us'd by the Butchers here in England when they weigh their Meat, but some are Bigger, some less as their occasions require.

They had no Names for Numbers before the Dutch came here, but they sufficiently declar'd to one another what Number they meant by their Signs and Fingers; but because the Dutch did not understand this way of Reckoning, they perswaded us to invent names to Signify Numbers which now we use after the same Manner as they do, proceeding from One to Ten, from Ten to Twenty, and so to a Hundred, a Thousand, &c. As appears in this example.

1	2	3	4	5	6
Tausb	*Bogio*	*Charhe*	*Kiorh*	*Nokin*	*Dekie*
7	8	9	10	11	11
Meni	*Thenio*	*Sonio*	*Kon*	*Amkon* or *Tauskon*	

12	13	14	15
Bogiokon	*Charhekon*	*Kjorhkon*	*Nokikon*

16	17	18	19	20
Dekiekon	*Menihm*	*Thenikon*	*Soniokon*	*Borhny*

2	1	2	2

after this *Borhny-taus* or *am Borhny Bogio*, and so on to

30	40	50	60	70

so on to *Chorhny Kiorhny Nokiorhny Dekiorhny Meniorhny*

80	90	100	1000
Theniorhny	*Soniorhny*	*Ptommftomm*	and *Ianate*,

so 1000, 2000. &c. And this may suffice for this Article.

CHAP. XXI

Of the Superstitious Customs of the Common People

THE COMMON PEOPLE are so much addicted to the Superstitious ways of foretelling things Future, that nothing happens to them either Ordinary or Extraordinary, of which they do not make a good or bad Omen, and Particularly they lay a great stress on Dreams; of all which I shall give some Instances, so far as I can Remember. If any one Dreams that he is at a Great Feast among Women, this Signifies that he has many Enemies, who are Contriving to kill him or do him some Mischief. If any one Dreams that he is bit or hurt by a Lyon, a Serpent, or some such Beast, he ought to have a care of a certain Enemy who will attempt to do him an Injury; but if he Dreams that he has kill'd a Wild Beast, then he thinks himself Secure from all Danger until a contrary Dream happens. If any one Dreams that one of his Relations or himself is Dead, they believe that God is angry with him, and therefore they usually consult the Priests what they are to do in this case, who always advise them to give something wherewithal to Atone their angry God. If any one Dreams that he has Lice, Gnats, or Ants, upon his Body, then they think that the Soul of some of their deceas'd Relations is detain'd in the Body of some Beast, (as was before-mention'd) and wants Money and other things; which they therefore take care to give to the Priests, that they may convey them to the Soul in distress. If any one dreams that he has lain with another man's Wife, then he is afraid lest some man lie with one of his Wives, and therefore he more narrowly observes them then at other times. And so much may suffice concerning Dreams.

They observe also other Omens, as the first thought that comes into their mind in a Morning after sleep, and the first Beast they see in a Morning. But then they say, if such a thing which comes into their mind do not strike their Fancy, the Omen concerns some other Body, but if it strikes the Imagination, then they apply it to themselves. There were a certain sort of men who pretended to explain very clearly all kinds of Omens for a very small Matter; but being for the most part mistaken in their Conjectures, the People complain'd of them to the Priests, who accused them to the Viceroy as Guilty of a Capital Crime, for which the Viceroy Condem'd them to Dye. And ever since the Priests alone Challenge to themselves the Priviledge, who so explain all sorts of Omens, that they can never be convicted of Lying in what they Say. For either they pretend that their God is well-pleas'd, or that he is angry with such a Man, or that the Souls of some of his Deceas'd Relations want Money, or that in the same Instant when they saw such an Omen the Soul of some of his Relations was Transform'd into a Star; all which the People do easily believe, who are therefore perswaded by the Priests to acquaint them with all the Omens they meet with.

And here I shall briefly relate a Notable Story concerning this Matter. A certain Rich Countryman being much Addicted to this kind of Superstition, had us'd for a long time to consult the Priests, who were wont very often to expound his Omens of the Need some of his Relations Souls stood in of Money, because he was Rich. The Countryman at last grew weary of such expensive Enquiries, and thought he had given Money enough to Redeem all the Souls that belonged to the Isle, and therefore contriv'd a way to cheat the Priest: For which end he went and told him, that in the Morning he had seen in his Garden more than a 100 Birds Singing, which after a short stay Flew away. But the Priest told him, If these Birds had continued a Longer time in the Garden, then for certain the Souls of your Deceas'd Relations had been Transform'd into Stars, but

A DESCRIPTION OF FORMOSA"

their sudden departure Signified that they still wanted something,
which being Furnish'd, then, says he you may see them, this night
ascending into Heaven; For which end you must give me so much
Gold so much Rice, and so much of other Commodities, and then
you may remain two hours upon the Roof of the House, and you
shall see the Stars, as it were, moving themselves, which are the
Souls signified by the Birds you saw in the Garden. The Countryman, tho' much against his Will, gave the Priest what he demanded,
and perhaps did still believe that there was something of Truth in
what he said; and therefore he went up to the top of his House,
and as the Priest had said, he saw the Stars moving themselves; but
having continu'd there all night, he observed a great Multitude of
Stars thus moving. And this observation he renew'd every night for
a whole week, untill at last he reckoned more Stars thus moving,
then the Number of Men who were known to be Dead in the whole
Island for the space of three Years amounted to: Whereupon he
went to the Priest and told him of it, and the Priest, perceiving
that he had detected the imposture, carried him before the chief
Sacrificator, who carried them both before the High Priest, or
their Pope, who upon hearing the whole matter condemned the
Priest to perpetual Imprisonment, because he had expos'd to
the Country-man the Mistery of Transforming Souls into Stars,
but condemned the Countryman to death for not yielding due
Deference and Submission to the Priest; from whence every one
may clearly perceive, what Tyranny the Priests exercise over the
common People, who are not permitted to declare Publickly any
doubt they have even of those things they know to be false. I could
add several other things to the same purpose, but that I think they
will be Tedious to the Reader; as the Noise which is made by the
Dogs when they Bark aloud or Houle, the Crowing of a Hen like
a Cock, the time when the Serpents hiss in the Fields, when the
Bears do not go out of the Wood, when the Eagles sit upon some

Turrets, Houses or Trees, all of which are interpreted to be good or bad Omens. But I have said enough of these Fopperies.

CHAP. XXII

Of the Diseases in Formosa and their Cures

THE GREATEST DISEASE to which the Natives are Subject is the Plague, which they believe does not proceed from Natural Causes, but from the common consent of the Sun Moon and Stars, who agree in sending it for a Punishment to Men, and therefore they rather make use of Sacrifices than Medicins for the cure of it. This does not happen frequently, for 'tis now 170 years, since there was a Plague in Formosa, if we may believe their written Books and Tradition. One Custom they have during the time of the Plague which is very remarkable; They ascend to the Tops of the Highest Mountains, that at other times are not Inhabited for the thinness of the Air, which is then accounted very wholesom; and there they seek out a Fountain of Water, of which they drink to excess, Eating nothing but herbs and certain Fruits: And this they continue to do till they think that the Plague is ceas'd, and then every one returns to his own House.

As to other Diseases which are very common here, as the Gout, the Tertian and Quartan Ague, they are not at all known there, yet they are sometimes, but very seldom, troubled with burning Fevers; at other times they have a pain in the Head or Stomach, but it lasts not long. If at any time they find themselves indispos'd, or any Disease coming upon them, they commonly use this Method for a Cure. They run 2 or 3 Miles as swiftly as they can, and in the mean time one prepares a Potion for him that runs, made of some Herbs and Roots, which he drinks off, after he has run his Race, while he is very hot, and Immediately goes to Bed, where he sweats till he has cured the Disease. And besides, their temperate way of Living conduces very much either to prevent or cure their Diseases, especially when they take Tobacco, which purges the Head and Body of ill humours. Here in England the generality of People frequent Taverns or Alehouses, and the constant custom of Drinking such Liquors as are sold there, proves prejudicial to the Health; but in Formosa they commonly spend their Idle hours, in Walking or Chatting together, and Smoking a Pipe of Tobacco; and if they drink any thing, it is only a dish or two of Tea or Chila, which if it does not any good, at least is no ways hurtful to the Health: And hence it comes to pass, that Men generally Live longer there than they do here, and free from many diseases to which Englishmen are liable. 'Tis a mistake to think that the Air alone will preserve our Health, unless we be also Temperate in Eating and Drinking; And this I have found true by experience, that no distinction of Climates has ever deprav'd my Temper and Constitution of Body, but by the help of Temperance I have still preserved my Health, thanks be to God, not only in my own Country, but in all the other Countries thro' which I have Travelled. But to return to the diseases of Formosa, the small Pox is very rife there, and scarce one escapes them; but they have them commonly whilst they are very young as in the 1st. or 6th. Month, or the 1st. or 2d. Year after they are Born, but they very seldom have them after they are three Years old, neither do I remember that I have ever heard of one that died of that disease.

After the Small-pox, there commonly Succeeds a certain Disease which we call Schimpyo which is only a Redness of the Flesh, together with a great Internal heat: And the Infants which are troubled with this Disease run the hazard of Death, unless they be kept at a distance from a Serene Air, and must live in places that are very warm until they becur'd. But these 2 Diseases Incident to Children last no longer than 3, or at most 4 Weeks.

Colicks are also very frequent in Formosa, in which the pain is sometimes so Intolerable that some kill themselves, others Command another to kill them.

Women in Child-bed are in great danger of Death. Which I think proceeds from want of Exercise, because when they are with Child they never Stir out of the Chamber, but sit and Work there all the day long: Many of them die before they bring forth, or if they escape Death yet at least they are Cruelly Tormented with pains, which some of them endure for a whole Month before they are brought to Bed.

Maids, for the most part, when they come to be 18 or 20 years Old, are troubled with a certain Disease, which we call Chatarsko, and here in England, is called the Green-Sickness, which makes them Melancholy, and destroys all their appetite to any thing except Matrimony, corrupts the Blood, and makes them palecolour'd. This Disease is peculiar to the Female Sex, for which there is no other Remedy but Marriage.

These are all the Diseases which I can Remember; but there may be others unknown to me. I will conclude with this General Observation, that both Men and Women, for the most part, die rather of a great Old Age, than of any other pains, except in Child-bearing and fits of the Colick; and you may frequently see Men a 100 years Old, without Labouring under any grievous Disease. If any ask me whether there be any such thing as the French-pox there, I answer I never heard of any such Disease, and probably there is no such thing in Formosa; because they allow Polygamy and prohibit Adultery.

CHAP. XXIII

Of the Revenues of the King, the Vice-Roy, the General of the Army, and of all others in high Places of Power and Trust

THE KING, BESIDES the third part of the Gold and Silver dug out of the Mines, which is paid him by the Vice-Roy, as has been observ'd in the Chapter of Metals, receives also from the Emperor of Japan 400000 Copans; out of which Revenue he is to pay 15000 Japan Soldiers above mention'd, his own Guards, and to maintain the Port of his Court. The Carillan or General has every Year about 70000 Copans. The Vice-Roy has 168760 Copans; out of which he pays to the Gnotoy Bonzo, or the High Priest, 50000 for himself: To the seven Gnotoi, Tarhadiazos, or chief Sacrificators 7700: To the four Governours of the four Isles 3600, viz. to each of them 900: To the six: Governours of the six Cities 3000, viz. to each of them 500: To the sixteen Governours of the Villages and Towns 4000, viz. to some of them 300, to others 250, and to others 200. But the Secular Priests are maintain'd by the People. After all which Disbursements, there remains in the Hands of the Vice-Roy 100460; out of which he is to pay his Soldiers, and all Officers employ'd by the Government, as Searchers, Guards, and such-like: But this Revenue of the Vice-Roy is not always a certain stated sum, for sometimes he receives more, sometimes less; but the others above-mention'd receive always the same Salaries.

This Revenue of the Vice-Roy arises partly from the Mines, partly from a Tax of a fifth part of all Goods, which is paid by

Merchants, Countrymen, and all others who have no Office under the Government, and is call'd Tuen Koon Bogio, i.e. two parts out of ten; and from another Tax which is rais'd upon all Goods exported and imported, which is call'd Tuen Dekie Bogio, because they pay a third part of the Vice-Roy.

CHAP. XXIV

Of all the Fruits of the Ground

No Corn, such as Wheat and Barley does grow in the Isle Formosa; and the reason of it is this, because the Sun being very hot, the Soil is sandy and dry, and so the Grain is dry'd up, not having sufficient moisture, before it is fully ripen'd: But instead of Corn they make use of Roots to make Bread withal. There are two Roots of which they make Bread, whereof one is call'd Chitok, and the other Magnok: Both these Roots are sown like RapeSeed, and when they are grown ripe they are as big as a Man's Thigh. These Roots grow twice, and sometimes thrice in a Year, when it is a good season; and as soon as they are fully ripe, they are cut off and laid in the Sun to be dried, and when they are dried they are cut in pieces and ground into a kind of Flower: And then this Flower being mix'd with Milk, Water, Sugar and Spices, is bak'd: and so it makes a very good sort of Bread, which is as white as Snow, and is call'd by the Natives Khatzadao. They have Bread also made of Wheat, which is brought thither from Foreign Parts; but that is too dear for the common sort of People. They have a kind of Bread also made of Rice boil'd with Saffron, which Bread is like an English Pudding, and is call'd by the Natives Kdekh; but this Bread will not keep like the former.

They have Vines also, and make Wine of the Grapes in some few places; but this Wine is not so sweet as the Spanish Wine in Europe; from whence they have that and other Wines, and also Ale, brought thither by the Dutch; but they are very dear, and are not so much lov'd by the Natives as they are by the Europeans. They have many other kinds of Drink, as Armag-nok, Puntet, Charpok, Chilak, Caffe and Tea. Ar-mag-nok, i.e. the fellow of Magnok, because these two are an agreeable mixture for health, which Liquor is made after this manner. They boil a great quantity of Rice in spring Water till it grows very thick, and then they make Balls of it as big as a Man's Fist, which they dry in the Sun, and then boil them in fresh spring-Water; and when it is boil'd enough, they put it into great earthen Vessels, and let it ferment, and after that, it is as strong or rather stronger than English Beer; and the longer it is kept the stronger it grows. Puntet is a Liquor that runs from some Trees, which they tap at a certain season of the Year: And the Liquor that comes from them they receive into Vessels, and mix it with Sugar, and then having kept it for some time, it has the same taste as soft Ale made of Oat-Malt. Charpok is the name of the Fruit of a Tree, and of the Liquor that comes out of it: The Tree is like a Wall-nut Tree, but in this differs from all other Trees, that whereas their Fruit hangs downward, the Fruit of this stands upright. The   Fruit in shape and bigness resembles a Gourd, and when it is ripe, it is cut off and pierc'd through, that the Liquor may run out of it, which is very strong; for if it be not press'd, the Liquor is more intoxicating than distilled Waters, or Brandy-Wine. Chilak. is a kind of a Powder made like Coffee, and is boil'd after the same manner, either with Milk or Water; but in this it differs from Coffee, that it may be drunk cold, whereas Coffee is always drunk hot. Tea and Coffee are of the same sort, and the Liquors are made after the same manner there as every-where else. Besides these Liquors they have many other sorts: Such are the Bullan, which is made of Apples and Pears, or of Oranges and Lemmons, and another Liquor, which is made like the Orgeat of the same Materials: And lastly, they who can get no other Liquor drink Milk and Water.

Besides all sorts of Fruits which are to be found here in England, as Apples, Pears, Cherries, Nuts, Plums, &c. they have many other things, such as Oranges, Lemmons, Sugar in great quantities, and

"A DESCRIPTION OF FORMOSA"

Spices, as Pepper, Cinamon, Cloves, Nutmegs, Tea, Coco's, Coffee, and the like, which are either wholly wanting here, or at least grow very rarely in England. Their Trees bear twice in a Year, and the Fig-tree three or four times: And these Fruits ye have here of the same kind with theirs, are not half so good or so great, or so well-tasted; so that the Ground there seems to have a peculiar virtue for ripening and improving the Fruit, which here it has not. As for instance, ye have here the same sort of Trees, which are there call'd Puntet; but pierce these Trees here when you will, and ye will find they will not run the 20th part of the Liquor which they yield there, neither is it so well-tasted. And this is confirmed by the experience of many.

CHAP. XXV

Of the Things which they commonly eat

BESIDES BREAD and Fruit, of which we have spoken already, they eat also Flesh, but not of all sorts of Beasts, for the Flesh of several Beasts, as has been formerly observ'd, is forbidden: But they are permitted to eat of Swine's Flesh, of all sorts of Fowl, except Pigeons and Turtles; of all sorts of Venison, except the Hart and the Doe, of all the Fish that swims in the Sea or the Rivers without any exception. They some times roast or boil their Flesh, but they know not what it is to stew any Meat, and therefore do not use it, though it is not forbidden. They commonly eat the Flesh of Venison and of Fowls raw: And, which may seem strange here in England, they eat Serpents also, which they look upon as very good Meat and very savoury, being broil'd upon the Coals: But before they eat them, they take care to extract all the Poison out of them, which they do after this manner: They take them when they are alive and beat them with Rods until they be very angry; and when they are in this furious passion, all the Venom that was in the Body ascends to the Head, which being then cut off, there remains no more Poison in the Body, which may therefore be safely eaten. They feed also upon Hen-eggs, Goose-eggs, and the like, and all sorts of wholesome Herbs and Roots.

CHAP. XXVI

Of the Animals in Formosa, which do not breed here in England

GENERALLY SPEAKING all the Animals which breed here, are to be found in Formosa; but there are many others there which do not breed here, as Elephants, Rhinocerots, Camels, Sea-Horses, all which are tame, and very useful for the service of Man. But they have other wild Beasts there which are not bred here, as Lyons, Boars, Wolves, Leopards, Apes, Tygers, Crocodiles; and there are also wild Bulls, which are more fierce than any Lyon or Boar, which the Natives believe to be the Souls of some Sinners undergoing a great Penance: But they know nothing of Dragons or Land-Unicorns, only they have a Fish that has one Horn: And they never saw any Griphons, which they believe to be rather fictions of the Brain than real Creatures.

Besides the Animals abovementioned, they have also familiar Serpents, which they carry about their Body; and Toads which they keep in their Houses to attract all the Venom that may happen to be there; and Weasels for eating of Mice, and Tortoises for their Gardens. There is also a kind of Animal much like a Lizzard, but not so big, which the Natives call Varchiero, i.e. the Persecutor of Flies; its Skin is smooth and clear like Glass, and appears in various colours according to the situation of its Body: 'Tis wonderful to see how eagerly and industriously it pursues the Flies wheresoever it sees them, upon a Table, or on Flesh, or in Drink, and it seldom fails of catching them. This kind of Animal is to be found only in Japan and America, besides the Isle Formosa.

"A DESCRIPTION OF FORMOSA"

Though the foresaid Animals do not breed here in England, yet they are too well known here to need any particular description.

CHAP. XXVII

Of the Language of the Formosans

THE Language of Formosa is the same with that of Japan, but with this difference that the Japannese do not pronounce some Letters gutturally as the Formosans do: And they pronounce the Auxiliary Verbs without that elevation and depression of the Voice which is used in Formosa. Thus, for instance, the Formosans pronounce the present Tense without any elevation or falling of the Voice, as Jerh Chato, ego amo; and the preterperfect they pronounce by raising the Voice, and the future Tense by falling it; but the preterimperfect, the plusquam perfectum, and paulo poft futurum, they pronounce by adding the auxiliary Verb: Thus the Verb Jerh Chato, ego amo, in the preterimperfect Tense is Jeruieye chato, Ego eram amans, or according to the Letter, Ego eram amo; in the preterperfect Tense it is Jerh Chato, and the Voice is raised in the pronunciation of the first Syllable, but falls in pronouncing the other two; and in the plusquam perfectum the auxiliary Verb viey is added, and the same elevation and falling of the Voice is observ'd as in the preterit. The future Tense of Jerh Chato is pronounced by falling the Voice in the first Syllable, and raising it in the rest; and the paulo poft futurum is pronounced after the same manner, only adding the Verb Yiar, as Jerh viar Chato, ego ero amo. But the Japannese say, Jerh Chato, Jerh Chataye, Jerh Chatar, pronouncing the auxiliary Verb always after the same manner. The Japan Language has three Genders; all sorts of Animals are either of the Masculine or Feminine Gender, and all inanimate Creatures are of the Neuter: But the Gender is only known by the Articles, *e.g. oi, hic, ey, haec,* and *ay hoc*; but in the Plural number all the three Articles are alike.

They have no Cases, and they use only the singular and plural Number, but not the Dual: As for example, *oi banajo, hic homo, os banajos, hi homines*. But since I do not intend to write a Grammar of the Language but only to give some Idea of it, it may be sufficient to add this general Observation, That it is very easy, sounds musically, and is very copious. If any one shall ask from what Language it is deriv'd? I answer, That I know of no other Language, except that of Japan, that has any great affinity with it; but I find many Words in it, which seem to be deriv'd from several other Languages, only changing either the signification or termination.

The Japannese wrote formerly in a sort of Characters most like those of the Chineses; but since they have held correspondence with the Formosans, they have generally made use of their way of writing, as more easy and more beautiful; insomuch that there are few now in 'Japan who understand the Chinese Characters.

But here it is to be noted, that the same Prophet Psalmanaazaar, who delivered the Law to the Formosans, did also teach them this way of writing, as is commonly believ'd.

They use only twenty Letters in their Language, which are to be read from the right Hand to the left; whose Names and Figures are as follows.

They have many particular Rules, as to the use of these Letters, which it would be endless as well as useless here to set down, and therefore I shall only add the names of some things that are most common, and subjoin to them the Lord's Prayer, the Creed, and ten Commandments in that Language, to give the Reader some Idea of it.

The Emperor is call'd in that Language, Baghathaan Cheveraal, i.e. the most high Monarch; the King, Bagalo, or Angon: the Vice-Roy, Bagalendro, or Bagalendtr; the Nobles, Tanos; the Governours of Cities or Isles, os Tanos Soulletos; the Citizens, Poulinos; the Countrymen, Barhaw; the Soldiers, Plessios; a Man, Banajo; a Woman, Bajane; a Son, Bot; a Daughter, Boti; a Father, Pornio; a Mother, Porniin; a Brother, Geovreo; a Sister, Javraijn; Kinsmen, Arvauros; an Isle, A'IJia; a City. Tillo; a Village, Casseo; the Heaven, Orhnio; the Earth, Badi; the Sea, Anso; Water, Ouillo.

The reason why the Japan Language differs from that of the Chinese and Formosans, is this, because the Japannese being banish'd from China, settled in the Isles of Japan; upon which account they so much hate the Chinese, that they have chang'd all things they had in common with them, as to their Language, Religion, &c. So that there is no affinity between the Japan and Chinese Language. But the Japannese being the first Inhabitants of Formosa, brought their Language along with them into that Island, which is now much more perfect than it was at their first coming. Yet the Formosans preserve still the purity of their Language without any considerable alteration, whereas the Japannese are continually changing and improving it every Day.

But that the Reader may have some Idea of the Formosan Language, I have here subjoin'd the Lord's Prayer, the Apostles Creed, and the ten Commandments in that Language, printed in Roman Characters.

The Lord's Prayer
Koriakia Vomera

OUR *Father who in Heaven art, Hallowed be* Amy Pornio dan chin Ornio viey, Gnayjorhe *thy Name, Come thy Kingdom, Be done thy Will* sai Lory, Eyfodere sai Bagalin, Jorhe sai domion *as in Heaven, also in Earth so, Our bread* apo chin Ornio, kay chin Badi eyen, Amy khatsada

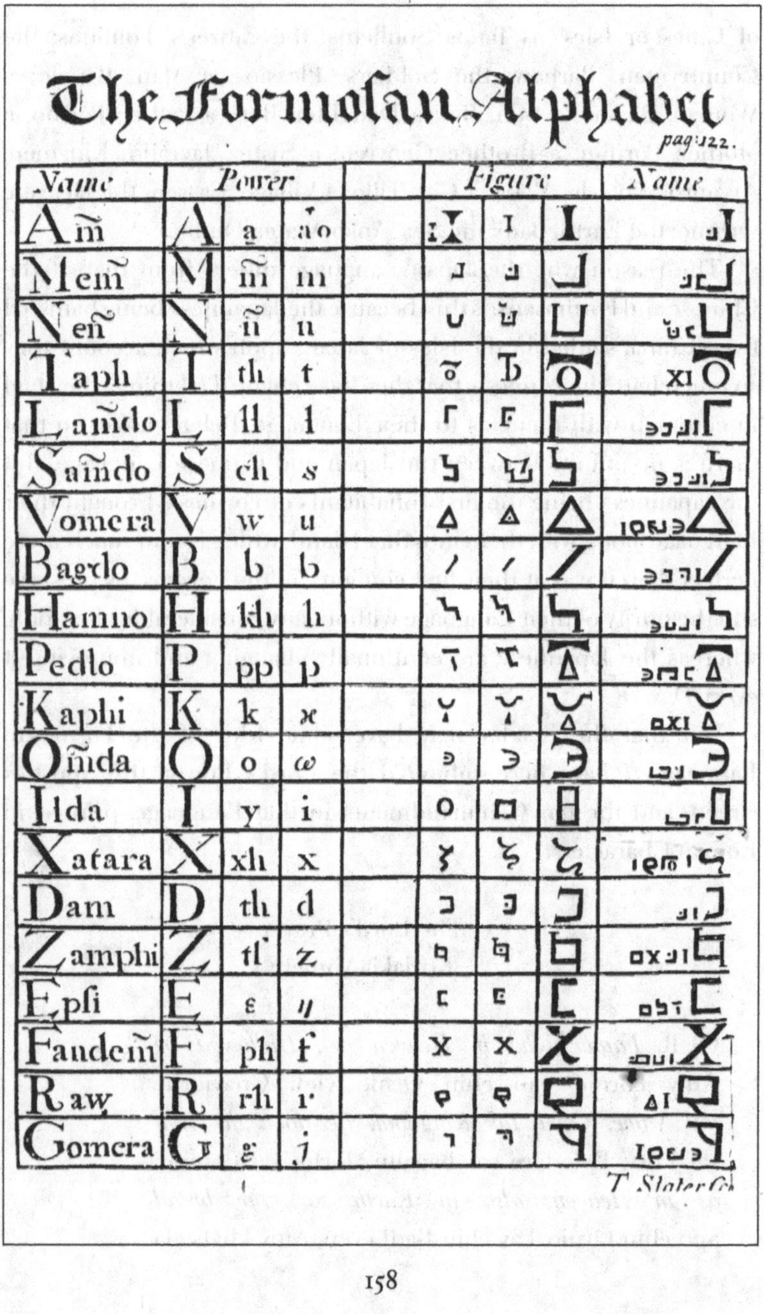

The Formosan Alphabet

pag:122.

Name	Power			Figure			Name
A m̃	A	a	ao	ɪ Ⅱ	I	I	ɪ
Mem̃	M	m̃	m	⅃	⅃	⅃	⅃⅃
Neñ	N	ñ	n	∪	ⱳ	⊔	ⱳⲥ
Taph	T	th	t	ⴀ	Ђ	ⴰ	xɪⴰ
Lam̃do	L	ll	l	Γ	Ⴀ	⌐	ⱯⱯ⊏⌐
Sam̃do	S	ch	s	Ⴄ	Ⴄ	Ⴄ	ⱯⱯ⊏Ⴄ
Vomera	V	w	u	△	△	△	ɪⱯⱭⱯ△
Bagdo	B	b	b	⁄	⁄	⁄	ⱯⱯ⊏⁄
Hamno	H	kh	h	⅂	⅂	⅂	ⱭⱯⱯ⅂
Pedlo	P	pp	p	⊤	⊤	△	ⱭⱭ⊏△
Kaphi	K	k	x	Ⴅ	Ⴅ	Ⴝ	Ɑxɪⴰ
Oñda	O	o	ω	Ⱶ	Ⱶ	Ⱶ	ⱵⱯⱱ
Ilda	I	y	i	o	▢	⊟	ⱱⱱⴰ⊟
Xatara	X	xh	x	�	Ⴝ	Ⴝ	ɪⱭⱱⱱ
Dam	D	th	d	⊐	Ⴅ	⅃	ⱱɪ⅃
Zamphi	Z	tf	z	Ⴄ	Ⴄ	⊡	ⱭxⱭɪⴰ
Epfi	E	ε	ıı	Ⴀ	Ⴀ	⊏	ⱭbⱭ⊏
Fandem̃	F	ph	f	X	X	X	ⱱⱱⱱX
Raw	R	rh	r	ᴘ	Ⴄ	⊡	△ɪ⊡
Gomera	G	g	j	ᴦ	ᴦ	ᴘ	ɪⱭⱱⱱᴘ

T Slater G:

daily give us today, and forgive us
nadakchion toye ant nadayi, kay Radonaye ant
our trespasses, as we forgive our trespassers,
amy Sochin, apo ant radonem amy Sochiakhin,
do lead us not into temptation, but deliver us from
bagne ant kau chin malaboski, ali abinaye ant tuen
Evil, for thine is the Kingdom, and Glory, and
Broskaey, kens sai vie Bagalin, kay Fary, kay
Omnipotence to all ages. Amen.
Barhaniaan chinania sendabey. Amien.

The Apostles Creed
I Believe in God the almighty Father,
Jerh noskion chin Pagot Barhanian Pornio
Creator of Heaven and of Earth:
Chorhe tuen Ornio kay tuen Badi:
And in Jesus Christ his beloved Son
Kay chin J. Christo ande ebdoulamin bot
our Lord, who concerved was of
amy Koriam, dan vienen jorh tuen
the Holy Ghost, born of Mary the
 gnay Piches, ziesken tuen Maria
Virgin, suffered under Pontius Pilate, was
boty, lakchen bard Poncio Pilato, jorh
crucified, dead and buried, descended
carokhen, bosken, kay badakhen, mal-fien
to the infernal places, on the third day
chinn xana Khie,   charby nade
rose from the dead, ascended into Heaven,
jandafien tuen bosken, Kan-fien chinn Ornio,
sitteth at the right hand of God

xaken chin testar-olab tuen Pagot
his Father almighty, who will come to
ande Pornio barhaniaa, dan foder
judge quick and dead
banaar tonien kay bosken.

  I believe in the Holy Ghost,
  Jerh noskion chin Gnay Piches,
  the Holy Catholick Church,
   Gnay, Ardanay Chslae,
  the Communion of Saints,
   Ardaan tuen Gnayji
  the Remission of Sins,
   Radonayun tuen Sochin.
  the Resurrection of the Flesh,
   Jandafiond tuen Krikin
  the Life Eternal. Amen,
   Ledum Chalminajey. Amien.

The Ten Commandments

Hear O Israel, I am the Lord thy
Gistaye O Israel, Jerh vie oi Korian sai
God who brought thee out of the Land of
Pagot clan bayneye sen tuen badi tuen
Egypt, and out of the house of bondage.
Egypto, kay tuen Kaa tuen slapat.
 I. *Not have another God before me.*
  Kau zexe apin Pagot oyto Jenrh.
 II. *Not make to thee a graven Image,*
  Kau Gnadey sen Tandatou
not an Image like to those things which in
kau adiato bsekoy oios day chin

Heaven are, or in Earth, or under the
Ornio vien, ey chin Badi, ey mal
Earth, not worship, not serve it, for
Badi, kau eyvomere kau conraye oion, kens
I am thy Lord God jealous, and I
Jerhvie say Korian Pagot spadou, kay Jerh
visit the sins of the Father upon the
lournou os sochin tuen Pornio janda los
Sons, until the third and f ourth genera
botos pei chin charby kai kiorbi Grebia
tion of those who me hate, and mer
chim dos oios dos genr videgan, kai teltul
cy I do to thousand generations of
da Jerh gnadou chin janate Grebiachim dos
them who me love, and my pre-
oios dos genr chataan kai mios belostos
cepts keep.
nautuo Iaan.

III. *Not take the name of God thy*
Kau chexner ai lory tuen Pagot sai
Lord in vain, for the Lord will not hold
Korian bejray, kens oi Korian kau avitere
innocent him who his name shall take in vain.
azaton oion dan ande Lory chexneer bejray.

IV. *Remember that thou sanctify the Sabbath;*
Velmen ido sen mandaar ai Chenaber,
Six days labour and do all thy work,
dekie nados farbey kai ynade ania sai Farbout,
but the sroenth is the day of
ai ai meniobi vie ai nade tuen
Sabbath of thy Lord, not labour in
Chenaber tuen sai Korian kau farbey chin

that day; thou not thy son, not thy daughter,
ai nade sen kau sai bot, kau sai boti,
not thy man-servant, not thy maid-servant, not
kau sai sger-bot, kau sai sger-botl, kau
the stranger who bef ore thy gates is, for
oi janfiero clan splan sai brachos viey, kens
the Lord created Hetl'Ven, Eearth, Sea
oi Korian chorheye Omio, Badi, Anso,
and all things which in them are in six
kai ania   dai   chin oios vien chin dekie
days, and on the seventh rested, therefore
nados, kai ai meniove stedellob, kenzoy
he blessed the seventh day and hallowed it.
oi skneaye ai meniobenado kay gnayfratayeoion.

     V. *Honour Father and Mother thine*
        Eyvomere Pornio kai Porniin soios,
that may be prolong'd thy days in land,
ido areo jorhen os os soios nados chin badi
which the Lord thy God shall give thee.
dnay oi Korian sai Pagot toye sen.

     VI. *Not Murder.*
        Kau anakhounie.

     VII. *Not Fornicate.*
        Kau verfierie.

     VIII. *Not steal.*
        Kau lokieyr.

     IX. *Not say a false testimony against thy*
        Kau demech stel modiou nadaan sai
Brother.
Geovreo.

     X. Not covet the house of thy Brother, not
        Kau voliamene ai kaa tuen sai Geovreo, kau

Covet   the wife   of   thy Brother, not
voliamene ey bajane tuen sai Geovreo, kau
covet   his man-servant or his maid-servant, or
voliamene ande sger-bot, ey ande sger-boti, ey
his oxe, or his ass, or whatsoever to him
ande macho, ey ande signou, ey ichnay oyon
belongs.
tavede.

The Kings Balcon

A Floating Village

CHAP. XXVIII

Of the Shipping of the Formosana

BESIDES THE SHIPS they have for making long Voyages into remote Parts, they have other Vessels which they call Balconos and Floating Villages, or Arcacasseos, which belong only to Noblemen, and are made use of by them to travel, or take their pleasure upon the River. The Emperor, the King, Vice-Roy, and the Noblemen, have every one a Balcon for himself, and a Floating Village for their Guards: Which Vessels will be best explain'd by the following Figures.

You must note, That there is no difference between the Balcon of the Emperor, a King, and a Vice-Roy, but that one is a little more magnificent than the other: The Arcacasseos or Floating Villages, in which are the Guards of him to whom the Balcon belongs, are all alike; only the others are not so long, not so broad and splendid as that of the King.

They have no Coaches to travel in by Land, but they have another kind of Carriage which is much more convenient, for they are carried by two Elephants or Camels, or Horses, in a thing like a Litter, call'd by the Natives Norimonnos, into which thirty or forty Men may enter; the Figure whereof is to be seen in the following Cut. All these Litters, whether they belong to Noblemen, or inferiour People, are made after the same manner, saving that some of them are more stately than others.

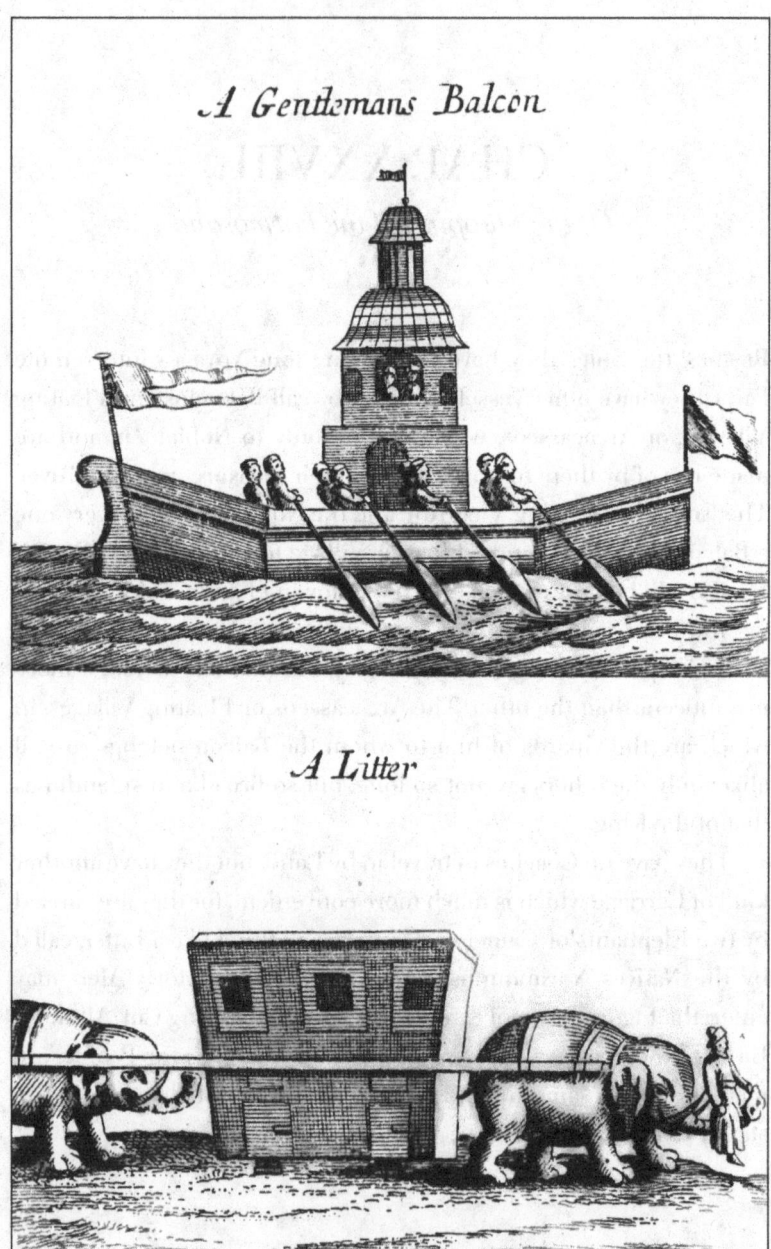

CHAP. XXIX
Of the Money of the Formosans

THE JAPANNESE have three sorts of Money. whereof some is made of Gold, and the other two sorts are of Silver and Brass. All these kinds of Money are current in the Isle Formosa; and besides them they have some of Iron and Steel.

The highest piece of Gold that's Coin'd at Japan is call'd Rochmoo, and is in value nine Copans and a half. A Copan is a piece of coin'd Gold worth seven Talos, and a Talo is a piece of Silver coin worth 58 Stivers, according to the Dutch way of reckoning, and very near worth an English Crown: But the Brass Money is of little value, as the Caxo, which are only worth about two Pence of English Money; and yet there are half Caxo: and quarter Caxo:; but this last kind of Money is only us'd in Japan and not in Formosa.

But in the Isle Formosa, a Rochmoo is valu'd only at eight Copans, and each Copan at six Talos, and a Talo at forty eight Stivers; not that these several pieces of Money weigh less in Formosa, for they are of the same weight, but because Gold and Silver is more plentiful there than in Japan: And besides them the Formosans have a piece of Steel Money, which they call Colan, and is of the same value with a Talo, though it is not so big. They have also Money made of Iron, which they call Riaon, a half Riaon and a quarter Riaon. Now a Riaon is worth fifteen Dutch Stivers. They have a little piece of Brass Money which they call Capchau, worth about seven Farthings. The Figures of all which may be seen in the following Table.

A Rochmoo which weighs eight pound and half of Gold, is of this shape. A is the upper part of it, whereon is the Head of the Emperor;

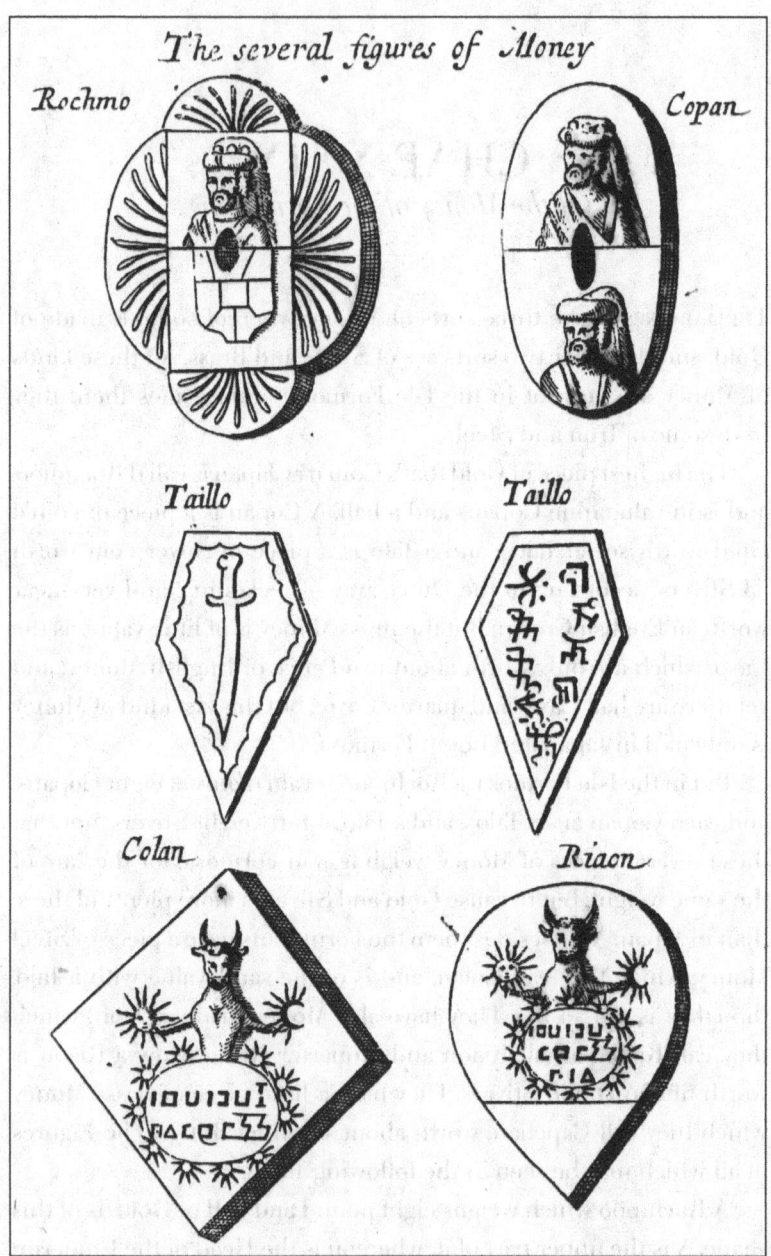

on the lower part of it are his Arms. But on the other side are the Arms of the King, who reigns in that Province where the Money is coin'd. There are also half Rochmoos of the same shape, and of half the weight.

A Copan is a piece of Gold which weighs one pound. In the upper part on one side it has the Head of the Emperor, and in the lower part the Head of the King: But on the other side it has their Arms. There are also half Copans; and both these sorts of Money have a hole in the middle.

A Talo is a piece of Silver Coin which weighs four Ounces, and on one side it has a Sword; and on the other are the ancient Characters of the Japannese, denoting its value.

Of the Caxo, some are round, others four squar'd and triangular; but these are coin'd only in Japan.

The Steel Money which is peculiar to the Isle Formosa, weighs one ounce and three quarters of an ounce. It is four squar'd, and is call'd Colan: On the one side it has the Arms of Religion, with this Inscription in Formosan Letters, Honour to God: And on the other side are the Arms of the King.

A Riaon is a piece of Iron Money, almost of the same bigness as a Kolan, and is worth fifteen Dutch Stivers. It has the same Inscription with a Kolan, but its Figure is almost round.

The Kapchau is a piece of Brass Money almost of the same value with a Japan Casiens or Caxa; its Figure is almost round, but it has no Inscription. There are also half Kapchaus and quarter Kapchaus.

CHAP. XXX

Of the Arms of the Japannese and Formosans

EVERY ONE I THINK knows that the Japannese use no such Arms as are commonly us'd here in Europe: But after the Jesuits and Dutch came there, they gave them some Guns and Muskets, which are not so many as to be serviceable to them in making War against their Enemies, but are laid up and kept as Curiosities to be shewn. The warlike Instruments which they make use of, are as follows.

First, the Battering-Ram, which is an Engine they make use of for destroying the Walls of a City. Fachos which are made of a certain tough Wood, to which are fastned many sharp plates of Steel, and are cover'd all over with Pitch, Rosin, and such-like combustible ingredients: And when it is kindled, it is thrown out of an Engin with so much force, that the sharp plates of Steel will cut three Men through the middle, standing directly behind one another. Next, they use in fighting long and short Spears, Bows and Arrows, and Cymiters.

This must be confessed by all that know them, that they are wonderfully skilful in all the ways of exercising their Arms, especially in shooting an Arrow, which they will direct as exactly to the Mark intended, as any European can a Bullet-shot out of a Musket.

They make Swords and Daggers so wonderfully fine, that they are highly esteemed in all the Eastern Countries. Metals are there so plentiful, and they are so skilful in melting and mixing, purging and tempering them, that in these arts of preparing Metal, they far excel the Europeans. Iron is the Metal of which the Japannese make their Swords and Daggers, of which they have one Mine; and their Swords are so curiously and exactly temper'd, that one of them is more precious than a Sword made of the purest Gold; for some of them are found to have so good an edge, that they will cut the biggest Tree in two with one blow, or divide a piece of Iron in two without blunting their edge. Their Daggers are made of such a mixture of Metals, that if any one be but slightly wounded with them, unless he cut off the wounded Flesh in the same instant, the wound becomes incurable. Of the same Materials they make the heads of their Lances, Arrows and Spears, so that their wounds are always mortal, unless the spreading of the Poyson be presently stopped; which practice seems to be unjustly condemn'd by the Europeans, since they themselves make use of more deadly Weapons than are usual there: Neither is it any great matter when we intend to destroy an Enemy, after what manner we kill him: Nay, in this respect the most deadly Weapons seem the best, because the more they kill, the sooner War is ended, which is the best for all parties.

However, all over the East the Soldiers formerly made use of these Japan Weapons: But now the Emperor has prohibited to export them under the pain of Death, so that none dare bring them into Formosa; yet the King who is sent thither has a Magazine full of these Arms, which are laid up for a time of War; and so they are far from being very rare and precious there: Nay, notwithstanding the prohibition, there are some who venture to export them clandestinely; for I remember I saw many of them in Goa, which are there publickly expos'd to Sale. They use also Slings, wherewith they throw Stones; this they do but very seldom.

CHAP. XXXI

*Of the Musical Instruments of the Japannese and
Formosans*

IT MUST BE ACKNOWLEDG'D that the Art of Musick was not known for
many Years in any of the Eastern Countries, neither had they any
certain method of singing and playing upon Instruments of Musick,
though they had then such as resembled the Drum and the Tabor,
the Trumpet and Flagellet, the Lute and Harp: But since the time that
the Europeans came thither, they have learn'd the way of making and
using these Instruments, which are now made almost after the same
fashion as they are here in England: For when they heard the Jesuits
play upon the Organs in their Churches, and sing Musically after
the manner of the Romish Church, they were mightily taken with
it, and inflam'd with a desire of learning the Art of Musick, which
now by their industry and ingenuity they have attained, tho' not in
perfection, yet to such a degree as wonderfully pleases themselves;
and therefore they commonly use both vocal and instrumental
Musick at their Marriages, Funerals, Sports and Recreations; and at
their offering Sacrifices, chiefly when they Sacrifice Infants.

Thus it is in Japan; but in the Island Formosa, the Natives still
observe their ancient method of singing and playing upon Musical
Instruments, if their way of singing may be call'd a method; for except
some few particular Prayers, which are sung by the Priests only, the
People sing all other things, every one after a different manner,
according to his fancy; which they do not look upon as ridiculous,
because they know no better; but on the contrary the different voices

and tones, which every one uses at pleasure, seems to them to make a pleasant harmony. After the same irregular manner they play upon the Instruments of Musick, which are us'd in Temples, such as the Drum, the Tabor, &c.

In which *A* is the Hand that strikes; *B* the Finger which makes the sound; *E E* the Skin or Parchment which is struck; *D D* the Plates of Gold or Silver, or some other Metal, which make a tinkling like a Gymbal. They use also the Harpsichord and Lute, Trumpets and Flagellets: but the Harp they do not use in their Temples. They have also Kettle-Drums, which make a harsh and warlike sound when they go to Battle; but they are so big that they must be carried by an Elephant. Other Instruments of Musick they have not.

CHAP. XXXII

Of the way of Educating their Children

I HAVE ALREADY SAID, that every Wife takes care of her own Children, but if she be the Wife of a Nobleman, she has Servant-Maids to look after them. They begin to teach a Child to read at three Years of age, and some of them will both read and write very well when they come to be five Years old; and from five to eight they instruct them in the Principles of Religion and Morality, and teach them how to behave themselves in company: After eight they send them to the Schools or Academies, which they do not before that time, because they think their Understanding is not ripe enough to apprehend such things as are taught there, tho many of them go to Schools before they are seven Years of age. The Mothers take a great deal of care in their Education, and their Fathers often examine them what progress they have made in their Learning: But their Parents never beat them, which they think improper, even when it may seem necessary to reform their manners, and deter them from the Vices to which they are addicted, (much less do they use such imprecations upon them as some Europeans do upon their Children,) but they instruct them the more carefully in their Duty, admonish them of their Faults, and by the most winning Persuasives exhort them to amend; for they hope that as their Reason encreases with their Years, they will of themselves abandon their Vices. And indeed this gentle method of Admonition and Exhortation does commonly prove so effectual, that young Men of six or nine Years of age will behave themselves with as much civility and modesty in their Discourses and Gestures as an old

Man can do, which deserves no small admiration.

They have a very sharp natural Wit, which readily learns the Languages and liberal Arts: And if any one think that I boast too much of my Countrymen, they may read the Account that is given of them in the Relations of several Authors.

When they are arriv'd at the fifth or sixth Year of Age, then their Parents send them to the School, and after that tho' they be negligent in their Studies, they never force them by threats to do any thing to mind their Book, but encourage them by good Words and fair Promises, and by proposing to them the Examples of others, either real or feign'd, who by improvement in their Studies have arriv'd at great Honours and Dignities; and by these and suchlike means they prevail more over the Youth, than they could by blows and menaces; for to speak the Truth, it must be confess'd, that the Natives of Japan and Formora, are naturally so stubborn and surly, that they cannot endure blows; and hence it often happens, that Servants when they are undeservedly and unmercifully beaten, will in revenge kill their Masters.

The Infants of Noblemen are carefully tended, and very carefully brought up by their Mothers and Nurses, who constantly attend them to see that they want for nothing, and cover them with Silk or Cotton to keep them warm; but never wrap them in swadling Cloths as the Europeans do: But their Country People are careless in cloathing their Children, and keeping them warm while they are Infants; and when they come to be two Years old, they suffer them to run naked over the Mountains, Meadows and Woods.

CHAP. XXXIII

Of the Liberal and Mechanial Arts in Japan

THOUGH THE JAPANNESE are inferiour to the Europeans in the Knowledge of the liberal Arts, yet this must be said for them, that as to all Arts whether Liberal or Mechanical, they excel all the other Eastern People. And though the Jesuits do mightily extol the Chinese above all the other Orientalists for their Ingenuity, yet I think they are much inferiour to the Japannese in sagacity and sharpness of Wit: for many of them, chiefly the Bonzii, spend their whole Life in studying; but their Wit for the most part consists in Riddles, Paradoxes and dark-sayings. They write many Books of Theology, which are chiefly design'd for the explication of their Articles of Religion, and the defence of their Idolatrous Worship: And in all their Meditations they chiefly apply themselves to the study of Philosophy, which with them is nothing else, but a collection of the Opinions of all the ancient Philosophers they know, which favour their own Superstition.

Altho' the Bonzii are bound to minister in holy Things, and by their office are peculiarly set apart for that service, yet they do not only study Philosophy and Theology, but Mathematicks, Medicine and Law; so that their Academies seem to resemble Universities here in teaching all the liberal Sciences. They teach also the Greek Tongue in the Isle Formosa, and every one may learn it in their Academies, who has Money enough to pay the Priests; but the Japan Bonzii teach it only among themselves, but not to the Laity.

These Colleges in which the Youth are taught, are endow'd with great Revenues; for all Princes, Noblemen and Gentlemen, send their Sons thither, and give great Gifts to them.

As to the Law, they have no Rules, but such as are discover'd by natural Light, or the dictates of Reason, or are founded upon the Authority of their Superiours, whose Will is a Law to their Subjects: Thus the Answer of the Prince decides any Controversie, and puts an end to the Suit of the contending Parties. But, as we have before observ'd, Meriandanoo made new Laws to restrain the Kings and Princes from enslaving their Subjects so much as they were wont to do.

The Physicians and Chyrurgeons in Formosa are very ignorant and unskilful, tho' they are very much honoured by all sorts of People. They know nothing of the art of Musick, as has been before observ'd: But as to the other liberal Arts, all the Sons of Citizens and Gentlemen study them in their Academies, provided their Fathers have sufficient means to maintain them there. They are excellent at making Verses, but chiefly the Bonzii in the Isle Formosa, who do not only compose Prayers, but also Sermons in Verse. They mightily affect Brevity in all their Writings, and labour only to express in a few Words the substance of any matter of fact, without taking notice of many Circumstances which set off the History: And therefore when they write Libels to any Prince, they contrive them wonderful short, yet so that nothing which is pertinent to the matter or substance of the Libel is omitted. Some of them are great lovers of Eloquence, but chiefly the Bonzii, and practise it very much in their Sermons, the better to move the Affections of their Hearers, and persuade them to do what they have a mind to.

The Japannese did formerly write from the top down to the bottom: Which way of writing they learn'd from the shape of a Man, whose Head is the highest part, and the Feet the lowest. But after that Meriandanoo had once obtain'd the Isle Formosa, and annex'd it to the Empire of Japan, the Japannese seeing the way of writing that was us'd by the Formosans to be much better and more easy, have ever since continued to write after that manner: And this they do so generally, that none but the Bonzii understand the ancient way of writing; for the rest are altogether ignorant of it.

Hitherto I have treated of their liberal Arts, I shall only add a few Words of their mechanical Arts. The Formosans have Painters who draw fine Pictures with great Art and Skill; and their Engravers are very famous for working both in Wood and Stone.

They have also Potters, who are very curious in making Dishes, which they call Porcellane, and the English China-Ware; and 'tis very well known, that in this Art they excel the Chinese and all the oriental People. But they have no Shoe-makers, Brewers or Bakers there; neither do they know the way of making Candles as you do here; but instead of them they use Lamps, with Oil, Links and Torches, made of the Pine-tree; and the Country People kindle Straw, or any kind of Wood which will flame and give light. The art of making Glass is not known over all the East, and when it was first brought to Japan, it appear'd to the Natives so admirable for its clearness and transparency, that the Mariners would sell a piece of Glass worth no more than a penny here for half a Copan; but now since Ships have frequently arriv'd in these parts, the value of them is very much fallen; and yet they cost twenty times more there than here. Some Noblemen have Glass-Windows in their Houses, but these cost so much that they are very rare, for the generality of the Natives use a thin waxen Silk-stuff, or Paper made of Silk, for their Windows, which they receive. from the Chineses. Their chief Arts are the Potters art, and the art of working with the Needle, in which they are ingenious to admiration: But above all they excel in the art of purging and preparing Metals, as has been observ'd in the Chapter of their Arms. And lastly, their Husbandmen are skilful enough in ordering and improving the Ground, according to the nature of the Soil.

And here it is to be noted, that all Artificers, and such as get their livelihood by their labour, are very little esteemed: And the Shopkeepers the richer they are, are so much the less valued, because they believe they must use many Lyes in commending and putting off their Merchandize, to encrease their Gain and Riches: And because the Japannese abhor a Lye, therefore they despise the Shopkeepers, whom they look upon as great Lyars; as the English despise the Mountebanks, who tell many Lyes of the Operations of their Medicines, which they sell upon a Stage. I shall only add, that as to other Mechanical Arts which are us'd here in Europe, the Natives are always learning something new from the Hollanders, having a very sharp Wit, which easily apprehends any Arts they once see.

CHAP. XXXIV

*Of the Splendid Retinus that attends the Vice-Roy of
Formosa when he goes to wait upon the Emperor*

SINCE ALL KINGS have not the same Dignity and Revenues, but
some are more, some less rich and honourable, therefore every
one of Japan, the King's Subject to the Emperor of hath a Retinue
proportionable to his Dignity. But the King of the Isle Formosa being
sent from the Emperor, is therefore always attended by the Vice-Roy
and Carillan before they go to wait upon the Emperor. 'Tis the office
of the Carillan to give the Emperor that account of the Isle which is
made by the King; and the Vice-Roy relates as from himself the same
things which the King relates by the Carillan, viz. all things which
concern the Government, the Subjects or the Commonwealth.

The Vice-Roy of Formosa does usually travel twice a-Year to wait
upon the Emperor of Japan; and then he has his own Balcon, which
has been before describ'd, and thirty-six Balcons of the Noblemen,
who attend him: But the Carillan travels in the same Balcon with
the King, as being his Companion. Besides these Balcons there are
eighty floating Villages, in which are the Guards of the Vice-Roy
and Carillan, and the Litters or Palanquins, in which they travel
when they pass through the Island. All things are set in order when
they come to the Isle Xyphon; forty floating Villages go before, and
eighteen Balcons of Noblemen, then comes the Balcon of the Vice-
Roy, and after it eighteen Balcons of Noblemen, and last of all forty
floating Villages, whereof one or two belongs to each Nobleman.

In this order they make their Progress till they come to the Sea-

Port Town, where they are to Land, and then they all go out, and Noblemen go into the Litters which are carried ashore for them, and the Balcons remain there till the ViceRoy returns. There are thirty-six Litters which belong to the Noblemen, who accompany the Vice-Roy; and there is one for the Vice-Roy, with whom the Carillan travels to bear him Company. All the Litters of the Nobility are an Ell and a half in height and length, and are made of Wood, curiously adorn'd within and without with Silks and Tapestry, finely wrought with the Needle, with plates of Brass or Copper, and many Pictures, and are usually carried by two Elephants.

The Vice-Roy and Carillan travel in one Litter, which is two Ells and a half high, and three Ells long, and is carried by two Elephants: Inwardly it is adorn'd with Silks and Cloth of Gold, finely wrought with the Needle; and outwardly it is covered with most pure Gold. In this Litter, besides the Vice-Roy and Carillan, are one Nobleman and ten Ladies of Honour, which are branches of the King's Family: It goes in the middle of all the other Litters, and is guarded with Soldiers before and behind, and on both sides.

All things being thus dispos'd, they enter into the Emperor's Palace, where they continue for a Month, and then return into their own Country. The Emperor does them this Honour, as to send twenty of his Courtiers to receive them when they land at the Sea-Port Town, and as many to accompany them, in Litters guarded with Soldiers, when they return to the Sea-Port. And during all the time they stay at the Emperor's Court, he puts all kinds of Honour upon them; for he diverts them with Hunting, Sports and Comedies, and admits them to a hearing every Day for an Hour in a publick Assembly: And lastly, when they are to go away, he loads them with Gifts, and very honourably takes a farewel of them.

'Tis a part of the Office of the King of Formosa to accompany the Vice-Roy to the Sea-Port Town call'd Khadsey, where he takes Shipping, and to receive him at the same place when he returns, and

attend him as far as the Castle. And lastly, it is to be noted, that altho'
the Emperor gives him only the Title of Vice-Roy, who was formerly
King of Formosa, yet he does him greater Honour than any other
King of the Empire.

CHAP. XXXV

Of the Success of the Jesuits in propagating the Christian Faith in Japan, from 1549 to 1615. More especially of the Reasons of the terrible Slaughter that was made of them about the Year 1616. And of the Law prohibiting Christians under pain of Death to come into Japan.

Since my design is only to give an Account of the Isle Formosa. and to touch upon the Affairs of Japan so far as they have Relation to it; I shall not pretend to give a particular History of the various success the Jesuits met with in propagating the Christian Religion through the several Kingdoms of Japan, of which I have receiv'd no certain information. But in general I am very well assur'd, by the constant uncontroll'd Tradition of my Countrymen; that notwithstanding all the difficulties they met with, they made a wonderful progress in the conversion of that Empire between the Year 1549, in which Xaverius says he, first arriv'd at Cangoxima, and the Year 1616 or thereabout; for 'tis commonly believ'd in Formosa that in this space of time more than a third part of Japan was converted to the Christian Religion; and Tampousamma himself, who was Emperor of Japan in the said Year 1616.

Though many other causes might concur to promote the spreading of the Christian Religion in Japan by the Jesuits, of which I can give no particular account, yet I am very certainly inform'd that one thing which contributed very much to the propagation of it, was their proposing the Christian Religion, after such a manner as was most agreeable to natural Reason, and the Doctrines and Practices commonly receiv'd among the Japannese.

Thus the Jesuits taught them in their first Lectures, That there was but one God, the Creator and Governor of all things in Heaven and Earth, and demonstrated his Eternity and other Attributes by natural Reason; but said nothing of a Trinity of Persons in the Unity of the God-head, lest it should shock their Belief of the one true God. And as to Christ, they affirm'd that he was a Divine Vertue residing in a human Body, or a mighty Hero sent from God to reveal his Mind and Will to Mankind; and they enlarged upon the Holiness of his Life, the Reasonableness and Excellency of his Doctrine, the many Miracles he wrought for confirmation of it, and the bitter and painful Death he endur'd on the Cross for the expiation of the Sins of Mankind: All which were agreeable enough to the opinions the Japannese had conceiv'd of their pretended Heroes, That they had done many wonderful Feats, and endur'd great and lasting Pains to deliver their Followers from future Torments. But all this while the Jesuits said nothing of his being God and Man in one Person, but conceal'd that Mystery, as being too difficult for the apprehension of the Japannese, until a more convenient opportunity.

They taught the Japannese to worship the only true God, and his Son Jesus Christ, who was rais'd from the Dead by the Almighty Power of God, and ascended into Heaven, and was exalted in the humane Nature to all Power in Heaven and Earth, to assist and relieve his faithful Servants: which was agreeable enough to the notions they had of their Deified Men, such as Xaca and Amida, to whom they pray'd for Relief in all their Straits and Necessities. And as to the Worship of Images and Saints departed, there was such a perfect Harmony between the Jesuits and the Japannese, That they desir'd them only to change their Idols for the Images of Jesus Christ, the Virgin Mary, and other Saints of the only true God, and to continue the same way of worshipping and trusting to the Saints, as Intercessors with God for them, but not to offer Sacrifices to them.

They administered Baptism in the name of the Father, the Son and the Holy Ghost, as the Rite of admitting Men into the Christian Church, and never declared the Holy Ghost to be a Divine Person in the ever-blessed Trinity, but represented him as the Power of God.

They administred the Lord's Supper in commemoration of the Death of Christ, but never offer'd to explain the Mystery of Transubstan tiation, or the Sacrifice of the Mess.

And by this way of representing the Christian Religion, and concealing those Mysteries which are more difficult to be apprehended and believ'd, and the peculiar Absurdities of the Popish Doctrines, it appear'd to contain nothing but what was agreeable to natural Reason, and the Notions and Practices commonly receiv'd among the Japannese, and so it easily gain'd credit and spread mightily among the ingenious Japannese; especially being recommended by some peculiar advantages it has above all other Religions, as particularly by the full assurance it gives of a future state of eternal Life and Happiness.

But as this Artifice gain'd the Jesuits many Followers, while they conceal'd the aforesaid Doctrines, which they did for many Years, until they found their Party very strong and powerful: So when they declar'd them to the People, and impos'd them as necessary Articles of Faith, the Christian Converts murmur'd against them for changing the Religion they had formerly taught; and the Pagans, but especially the Bonzies exclaim'd against them as Impostors, for deceiving the People with new Devices, which occasion'd many to make defection from them, and rais'd in all a strong suspicion of their Insincerity: So that this Declaration of these new Doctrines prov'd very much to their disadvantage, and may be reckon'd one cause of their utter Ruin and Extirpation.

A second Cause was the great Envy and Indignation which all the Pagans, but chiefly the Bonzies, conceiv'd against the Jesuits, because they insinuated themselves so far into the favour of Kings and Princes, and all the rich Men who were Converts to their Religion, that they setled great Revenues upon the Christian Monasteries, which us'd formerly to be given to the Bonzies; nay, the Fathers disinherited their Sons to enrich their Monasteries, which so exasperated the Minds of the Pagans against them, that they endeavoured by all means to extirpate them.

A third Cause was the discovery of a Conspiracy, carried on by the Jesuits, to betray the Empire of Japan into the Hands of the King of Spain; for which end they had sent him Letters, which were found out, giving him an account of the situation of their Harbours, and of their several Cities, Castles and Forts, and the manner how they might be besieg'd and taken. The Jesuits confess, that the great Dominions which the King of Spain possess'd in the East and West Indies, gave the Japannese a great Umbrage; and this they say mov'd them to set on foot a design of abolishing their Religion, and driving them out of their Country: But they deny that they ever wrote such Letters to that King, giving him an account of the Strength of the Japan Empire, and the ways of attacking it; and pretend that these Letters were forged by the Hollanders, on purpose to render the Portuguese odious, and get their Trade in Japan out of their Hands. But this Forgery was never prov'd against the Dutch; and therefore 'tis commonly believ'd in Formosa, that the Jesuits were the Authors and Contrivers of the aforesaid Letters, which must certainly render them very odious to all the Pagans.

But all these three Causes were only preparatory to that which follows, which was the last and immediate Cause of the great slaughter of the Christians in Japan. For the better understanding of which we must consider, that in the great progress which the Christian Religion had made in Japan, by the preaching of the Jesuits and other Missionaries of the Romish Church, there were not only several Kings and Princes and many great Lords, but also an Emperor who had embraced Christianity, whose name was Tampousama; and he gave them not only a Toleration, but all manner of Encouragement to propagate and settle their Religion in all parts of the Empire. The Jesuits being puffed up with this success, and supported by so great an Authority, ventur'd boldly to expose their peculiar Dogmata of Transubstantiation, and the Sacrifice of the Mess, &c. which they required all the Christians to believe, under pain of Damnation; and to use all the pious Frauds they could invent, for draining the Riches of Japan into their own Coffers. And having by this means given great offence to the Christians, and incurr'd the great hatred of the Pagans, and raised a vehement suspicion in all sorts of People of their being Impostors; they began to be afraid, lest the Pagans should conspire together to work their Ruin, and therefore were resolv'd to be beforehand with them, and to take the shortest way for converting the whole Empire to their Religion.

To this purpose they forg'd a Lye, which they went and told the Emperor, That the Pagans were contriving to raise a Rebellion against him, and to cut the Throats of all the Christians. That they had already had several Consultations about carrying on this wicked Conspiracy, which they would certainly put in execution, unless they were timely prevented. The Emperor who look'd upon them as very wise Men, and put an entire confidence in them, asked them, what they would have him to do? To which they readily answered, That to secure himself and the Christians from this Conspiracy, he could do nothing better, than to send his Letters to all the Christian Churches, requiring the Christians every-where throughout the Empire, to rise up in Arms on such a Day, about a certain Hour of the Night, and kill all the Pagans: For by this means, continued they, the wicked Design against your Majesty and the Christians will be prevented, and the Christian Faith alone will flourish through all your Empire, and there will be none left alive to trouble you, or disturb the Peace of your Government. Besides, the better to excite the Emperor to this undertaking, they assur'd him that he was oblig'd to do it, not only in point of Policy, but of Religion, because this would be such a commendable and meritorious Work, to extirpate Heathenism and settle Christianity in all his Dominions, that he might certainly expect the Blessing of God, and of Christ upon himself, and all his Christian Subjects, for finishing such a glorious Design. But, added they, if you delay much longer to put it in execution, you will certainly find by woful experience, that your Majesty and all the Christians will be murther'd in one Night; the consequence of which must be the utter Extirpation of Christianity in Japan.

These Things they represented with so much seeming Zeal and affectionate Concern for the Christian Religion, that the Emperor was prevail'd upon, as is commonly reported, to grant them his Letters to be sent to all the Christians, requiring them to destroy all the Pagans in his Dominions; though others say that the Jesuits presum'd so far upon the Emperor's good Affection to their Cause, that they wrote these Letters in the Emperor's Name without his Knowledge, and dispatch'd them to all the Christian Churches. However this is certain, that all the Churches receiv'd Orders written in the Emperor's name, to rise up in Arms; on such a Day, at such an Hour of the Night, and destroy all the Pagans. And though this Design was managed with all the Artifice of the Jesuits, to conceal it until the time of execution, yet they could not carry it on so secretly but the Pagans came by some means or other to hear of it, time enough to prevent the fatal Blow: For either the Christians, who had Fathers or Mothers, or other near Relations that were Pagans, out of natural Affection to them, discover'd the Plot, that they might have an opportunity to save their Lives; or others being touch'd with an Horror of the Bloody Conspiracy against their Countrymen and Friends, found their good Nature too hard for their Religion; and therefore gave timely notice to the Pagan Kings and Princes to fortify themselves against the intended Massacre: Which they did so effectually, that having got all things ready, they rose up in Arms with their Pagan Subjects on the very Day before that in which the Christians were to put their Design in execution, and fell upon them, and destroy'd them with a very great slaughter wheresoever any Christians could be found. The Emperor being a Christian, and having too much countenanced the Jesuits in their intended Massacre, was forc'd by the Pagans to leave his own Dominions, and went into the City of Goa, where he died, and his Body is still preserved in the Church of the Jesuits, where a stately Monument is erected to his Memory, with an Inscription to this purpose, Here lies Tampousama Emperor of Japan, who was banished out of his Dominions, and died a Martyr for the Christian Religion. At the same time there were five Kings and two Vice-Roys apprehended, who had promoted the Christian Religion in their several Kingdoms; and they were thrown into Prison, and there remain'd until they died.[6]

The slaughter was so general, that not only the Jesuits and other Missionaries of the Romish Church, but all the Japannese that had been converted by them, were put to Death whensoever they were seiz'd; Some were hang'd, some thrown into the Rivers, or old Ditches, others were beheaded, and great numbers suffered the most cruel Deaths the Pagans could invent, But though the slaughter was very general, yet it cannot be imagin'd, that all the Christians were apprehended at the same time, but many of them lay conceal'd, and skulk'd up and down in Corners for several Years before they were discover'd; and after the first Heats of the Persecution were over, many of those Jesuits and Monks who were seiz'd, were for some time respited, and being cast into Prison, continued there until a new Emperor was Created, and then were put to cruel Deaths, with

---

6   The truth is that Francis Xavier arrived with other Jesuit priests in 1549 and were initially successful, with perhaps 100,000 converts in the southern island of Kyushu, including some of the local lords (daimyo). From the late 1500s, Christianity was actively suppressed. The Jesuits were thrown out in 1587 and Christianity was banned in 1620. It survived only with a small number of underground believers until the American "Black ships" under Commodore Perry arrived in 1856 to open up Japan to the outside world.

most exquisite Torments.

After this time the name of a Christian grew so odious through all the Empire of Japan, that no Christian was suffered to live in it, but the Pagans slew them all whensoever they discovered them. And this wicked and bloody Conspiracy, which was so contrary to the mild and charitable Spirit of Christianity, was such a Scandal to the Pagans, and reproach to the Christians, that henceforward they were all esteem'd Villains, Rebels, Impostors, and the worst of Men; and therefore when any of them were found out, all the People cry'd out, Away with them, Crucifie them: And Searchers were appointed to enquire diligently in all places, if any of them could be discovered; as has been already observ'd in the Chapter of Laws.

And this Relation of the Conspiracy of the Jesuits and other Popish Priests, against the Pagans, and the great Slaughter of the Christians, which follow'd upon the Discovery of it, is as firmly believ'd in Formosa, by Tradition from Father to Son, as the Gunpowder-Plot is believ'd here in England, to have been contriv'd by the Jesuits and other Papists: But I must confess, that I cannot positively determine the time when it happen'd; only I think it most probable, that it was about the Year 1616.

CHAP. XXXVI

*Of the coming of the Dutch into Japan, with their Success,
and the Tricks they play'd*

THE DUTCH HEARING of the great Slaughter of the Papists in Japan,
and that they were for ever banished from that Empire, laid hold
of this Opportunity to settle a great Trade with the Japannese; and
for that end having laded several Ships with great Stores of such
Commodities as they thought most vendible in that Country; they
sail'd to Japan, where being arriv'd, they were presently call'd to
an account, what they were? and from whence they came? They
answer'd, They were Hollanders; and when the Japan Inquisitors
urg'd them farther to declare, whether they were Christians or no?
They pretended at first they did not understand what they meant by
that Name, and therefore they could only tell them they profess'd
the Holland's Religion: But at last some of them told the Japannese,
That they had heard of some call'd Christians, who were Impostors,
and worshipped a Crucified Man: By which Character the Japannese
understood that these were the Christians who had formerly been
in Japan. And then the Dutch added farther, That there were none
such in their Country, but in other parts of Europe; and that the
Hollanders were so far from being of the same Religion with them,
that they had always been hated and persecuted by these Christians
upon the account of Religion.

These things being related to the Emperor, he commanded
that they should have leave to land, and to bring them before him:
When they were come into the Emperor's presence, they presented

him with two great Guns, and a striking Clock with an Alarm, and a musical Bell; both which wonderfully pleased the Emperor, but chiefly he admired the two Guns when he saw them charg'd and discharg'd before him: Whereupon he gave them free leave to come and import their Commodities into his Country, as thinking that their Commerce would be not only safe, but very advantageous to Japan. But after they had traded there for some Years, they begg'd leave of the Emperor to build a great Storehouse, in which they might lay up all their Merchandize; pretending it was a great loss to them to carry their Goods up and down the Country before they could sell them·; and that it would be more convenient, not only for themselves, but also for the Japannese to have a certain place appointed whither all Persons might resort, either to buy their Commodities, or take them in exchange for the Product of their Country The Emperor granted them leave to build such a House for containing their Goods: But they instead of a Ware-house, built a very strong Castle, with very good Fortifications; yet none of the Natives ever suspected them of any ill design, (but thought that the House was built after the Dutch way,) until some time after it was finish'd. But their design was discover'd when a new Fleet of Ships arriv'd from Holland in Japan; for these Ships were laden with Guns, Muskets, Pistols, and all sorts of Warlike Instruments, and great Stores of Gunpowder and Bullets; as plainly appear'd by this Accident: The Dutch having conceal'd their Arms and Ammunition in Wooden Frames, that they might not be seen by the Japannese, convey'd them out of their Ships, and laid them upon Carts to be carried to their Castle: But it happen'd, unluckily for them, that some of the Carts were broken by the way, and the Wooden Frames burst in pieces by the fall, which discover'd their hidden Treasure of Arms and Ammunition, and alarm'd the Japannese, who saw them, with the apprehension of some wicked Design, which was to be executed by such great quantities of Warlike Preparations: Whereupon some of them run presently and acquainted the Emperor with what they had seen, and the danger that threatned his Country by the Tricks of these deceitful Hollanders; and he sent away in all haste 10 or 12 Companies of Soldiers, who kill'd as many as they could find of them; but the greatest part of them had escap'd from the Castle, and were got into their Ships which had put to Sea, before the Soldiers arriv'd: which happen'd by the over-sight of the Natives, who might easily have encompass'd the Castle at some distance, so that none could enter in or go out of it, whereby all that were in it would have been forced either to surrender themselves or die for Hunger. After this their Castle and all the Guns they could find were seized by the Japannese for the use of the Emperor; and the Dutch were for some time prohibited any Commerce with Japan. But upon their humble Petition and fair Promises, the Emperor gave them leave to come into Formosa, which was then under his Dominion, and thither they resorted for some time: But the Hollanders not finding in Formosa all the Commodities they wanted, did again beg leave of the Emperor to trade into Japan; which the Emperor would not allow, until at last the King of Nangasak interpos'd on their behalf, and pray'd that he might be permitted to receive them into his Isle, which is not far distant from the rest of Japan. And this the Emperor granted upon the following Conditions, 1st, That they should trample upon the Crucifix. 2dly, That the Inquisitors should take out of their Ships all their Guns and Ammunition, all their Sails, Masts, Ropes and other Furniture, to be kept in a Store-house as long as the Dutch stay'd in the Country. 3dly, That he should appoint Soldiers to go along with them through the Country, and observe them. 4thly, That they should not stay any longer than the Emperor pleas'd; but as soon as he should send his Orders for their going away, they should make all things ready for sailing, and depart presently.

These Conditions have been hitherto very exactly observ'd, whenever therefore they have sold off, or barter'd all their

Commodities, and are ready to put to Sea again, then all their Warlike Instruments and Ship-Tackle, that were taken away at their first coming, are restor'd to them again, and they have free liberty to return into their own Country.

After the Dutch had got footing in Japan, and the Christians were prohibited to come there under pain of Death, the Dutch advised the Emperor to distinguish Christians from all other Foreigners by this Test, viz. by making an Image of Christ Crucified, which these Christians adore, and keeping it in all their Sea-Port Towns, and requiring all Foreigners to trample upon this Image: For, said they, If these Foreigners be Christians they will not trample upon it; And all others who do trample upon it, are certainly no Christians.

This Test was afterwards try'd upon some Jesuits, or other Monks of the Romish Church, who ventur'd to come into Japan, hoping perhaps to conceal themselves under the disguise of being Hollanders: But when they came into the Harbour, an Image of Christ Crucified was brought to them, and they were required to trample upon it, which they refus'd to do; whereupon they were all apprehended, being about 46 in number, and within a few Days crucified according to the Laws of Japan; and the Festival in Commemoration of their Martyrdom is celebrated by the Jesuits to this Day: But the Hollanders make no scruple to trample upon the Crucifix when-ever they are required to do it; and therefore they are not accounted Christians by the Japannese; according to the common opinion of all Japan, That those Foreigners only are Christians who refuse to trample upon the Crucifix.

CHAP. XXXVII

Of the new Devices of the Jesuits for getting into Japan

THUS THE HOLLANDERS, by denying Christianity, secur'd their freedom of Trade in Japan but the Papists were for ever shut out of that Country by this Test of Christianity, until the Jesuits by their subtilty invented a new way of procuring their admission into it, which was this: They learn in the first place the Japan Language in the City of Goa, where it is taught in the Academy; and when they can speak it very well, they put on the Japan Habit, and thus accoutred, they go to some Port in Japan, and being examined by the Searchers what Country they belong to, and from whence they come? They readily answer, That they are Japannese, and come from such an Island, and such a City in Japan, naming them, which is easily believ'd by the Searchers, because of their Language and Habit.

And having thus securely pass'd the Test, when they come ashore they disguise themselves under various shapes; for some set up for Merchants and Toy-sellers, others for Tutors; or Mechanicks, and they live in a private House, and follow their several Employments, with as much care and industry, as if they depended upon them for a livelihood, though 'tis certain they are otherwise provided with sufficient means to maintain them, by those who send them thither. For the Pope of Rome sends every Year a certain number into Japan, and takes care to furnish them with all things necessary, and they are allow'd two Years for learning the Japan Language, four Years for their stay in Japan, and about three Years for their Journey backward and forward. They have a certain Japan Word, which they pronounce after a manner peculiar to themselves, whereby they know one another; the Word is Abo, which in Japan signifies quickly, by which the new-comers, as they walk through the Cities and Villages, know their Brethren that have been there before them; and after they know one another, they meet together in private places to discourse about their own Affairs.

Thus there is a continual Succession of a new Missionary after four Years are expir'd, to supply the place of him who then returns home, as I am very well assur'd by my own experience, though 'tis not easy to guess for what end they are sent, or what good they do when they come there. For it is in vain for them to pretend that they convert many of the Natives, during their four Years stay, to the Christian Religion, as I know that some of them boast after their return, since it is impossible they should escape the diligence of so many Searchers, as are every-where appointed to detect them, if they should publickly own themselves to be Christians, and endeavour to convert the Pagans: And indeed, if it were true what they relate, that one had converted twenty, another thirty, and a third fifty, during their stay in Japan, ever since the time of their Banishment, there would be very few Pagans left in that Country, according to their account of Conversions. 'Tis true, that some Years ago there were Jesuits, or Popish Priests, who made some Converts to Christianity! but in a little time they were discover'd by the Searchers, and both they and their Converts were burnt alive, except a few who renounced Christianity and embraced their ancient Idolatry, for fear of the Torments of such a cruel Death: But at Rome they talk nothing of any such disasters, but every one boasts of the numerous Converts he has made in the Empire of Japan, and pleases himself with the Relation of his Travels, and the many wonderful things he has seen, being greatly puffed up with an Opinion of the great Glory and Fame he has merited by such a difficult and noble Undertaking. Upon the whole matter it seems to me most probable, that the great

Design of the Missionaries, who are sent to Japan, since the time of their Banishment from it, is to spy out the Country, and to inform themselves exactly of the Situation of their Harbours, the Number of their Forts and Castles, and all the Strength of the Empire, and to take Aim by what Methods they may be attack'd with best success, hoping that at length some magnanimous Christian Prince will undertake a glorious Expedition, with sufficient Forces to conquer that Empire by their direction, and to plant the Christian Religion among the Natives, in spite of all the Prejudices wherewith they are possess'd at present against it: For indeed I cannot perceive what other Benefit and Advantage they can propose to themselves by all the Trouble and Expences they are at, in sending so many Missionaries into Japan.

Within a few Years after the Persecution of the Christians in Japan, the Emperor having obtain'd the Isle Formosa, as has been above related, began to persecute also the Christians that were in that Country; but tho' he treated the Jesuits and Popish Priests there with the same severity he had us'd in Japan, burning some alive, crucifying others, or hanging them up by the Legs till they were dead; yet to the Natives who were Christians he shew'd more Mercy, leaving it to their own free Choice, either to renounce Christianity, or to depart for ever out of their own Country; whereupon many of them chose rather to fly into other Countries than deny Christ; but others being unwilling to leave their Estates and their Country, renounc'd Christianity, and embrac'd their former Superstition. And after that time the same Law was in force against the Christians in Formosa, as was made against them in Japan.

THE CONCLUSION

FROM WHAT HAS been said of the Causes of the great Persecution of the Christians in Japan, we may clearly understand how great a prejudice the Jesuits have done to Christianity, and what a Reproach and Disgrace they have brought upon the Christian Name, by imposing their Popish Errors upon the People as necessary Articles of Faith, and by contriving that barbarous and bloody Massacre which they intended against all the poor Pagans: Whereas if they had propos'd the Christian Religion in its purity and simplicity, and behav'd themselves towards their Proselytes with that Meekness, Charity, and Sincerity, which became their Apostolical Office, I dare be confident to affirm, that in all probability the whole Empire of Japan had now been Christian: But now by their Misrepresentations, and wicked Practices, the Japanese have such a false Notion of Christianity, and such strong Prejudices against it, that it would be much more difficult now to convert them; nay, the Door is shut against any Christians who might have such a charitable Design, or would attempt to remove their Prejudices, and possess their Minds with a just Idea of Christianity. How detestable then was the Wickedness of the Jesuits, which occasion'd all this Mischief. And how deplorable is the Case of these poor Pagans, who are now so fetter'd in Chains of Darkness, and bound up to their Idolatrous Practices, that they can never hope to see the glorious Light of the Gospel, or feel the Power of it in their Hearts and Lives, as might have been reasonably expected from them: For if they do so exactly observe the Precepts of their own Religion, altho' it be uncertain and contrary to the Divine

Nature, altho' it enjoyn them such a horrible and cruel Practice as to sacrifice their own Sons; with what Cheerfulness, Humility, and Veneration, would they have perform' d the rea sonable Service and Obedience of Christianity, had they been enlightened with that heavenly Doctrine in its purity, and tasted the Power of it, in purging their Hearts, and reforming their Lives.

Some perhaps may think that I have done too much Honour to the Pagan Religion as it is profess'd in Formosa, by giving such a long and particular Explication of it, as if I were still persuaded of the truth of it; which God forbid: And therefore I must desire such Persons to consider, that I was oblig'd to give an Account of all things relating to that Religion, as they are to be found in Jarhabadiond, which is our Scripture, tho' I am very far from believing them to be true; nay, I am fully persuaded that they are false, by the following Reasons which I shall briefly mention: 'Tis a certain and infallible Argument of the Falshood of any Religion, that it commandeth such things as are contrary to the Divine Nature, and to those Notions which every one hath of God's infinite Goodness: Such is the Command in our Jarhabadiond, which requires us to sacrifice so many thousand innocent Babes every Year; which is a thing so cruel, and so contrary to the Tenderness of Human Nature, that we cannot believe it to be the Command of a good and gracious God, but of some evil Spirit who delights in Human Blood, and in the Misery and Destruction of Mankind. And when once I was convinc'd of the Falshood of our Religion, by requiring such a cruel and bloody Sacrifice, I presently concluded, that all the Miracles pretended to be wrought in confirmation of it, were meer trick and forgery; because I am cetrain that God would not exert his Omnipotent Power to confirm a Lye, and maintain an Imposture. Besides that, any one may quickly be satisfied how little Reason there is to believe, that the pretended Miracles were really wrought, since they are only mention'd in our Jarhabadiond, which the Priests keep in their own hands, and will not suffer any of the common People to have a Copy of it; which gives a shrewd suspicion, that there is some Trick and Imposture, since they do so studiously avoid any means of discovering the Truth; which suspicion is very much increas'd by the Tyranny which the Priests exercise over the common People, in exacting an implicit Faith to their Dictates, without giving them any rational Grounds for believing, and obliging them under pain of Death never to accuse the Priests of any Falshood, tho' they be very certain that he is guilty of it. The Priests indeed pretend, that their God does sometimes appear to the People in the form of a Lion, when he is angry with them; and at other times, in the form of a Camel, when he is pacified: But every one may plainly perceive, that this pretended Miracle is nothing but a Trick of the Priests, who have the opportunity of shewing such or such a Beast to the People, without being discover'd, since the whole management of the matter is left to themselves, having the Beasts ready to set up at their pleasure with all secrecy. If any one should ask me, How can the Priests put such Tricks upon the common People, and carry on such Impostures? I answer, There are many Instances of the same nature in other Nations, who having no Revelation, believe and do such things as are more absurd than what is here pretended: Such were the Egyptians who were famous for all parts of Learning, and yet were persuaded to worship Crocodiles and Onions. Nay, even in the Roman Church we see, that many Absurdities are impos'd upon the common People to be believ'd contrary to Sense and Reason: And why then may not such a rude and ignorant People as the Formosans, be impos'd upon by the Tricks of cunning Men? But how this Imposture is manag'd, 'tis not my business at present to enquire, 'tis sufficient for me, that I am fully persuaded by undeniable Arguments of the Falshood of the Religion of Formosa. Now to this Omnipotent and Merciful GOD, who hath by the Grace of his Holy Spirit call'd me from Error and Superstition, to the true Know ledge of his Will, and of his Son Jesus Christ, my Redeemer and Mediator,

be ascrib'd eternal Praise, Honour, Magnificence, and Glory, by all
the Creatures for ever and ever. Amen.

Appendix

CONCERNING

The AUTHOR'S Journey from Avignon to Rome

IN THE YEAR 1701, being the Year of Jubilee, I was invited by the Jesuits to accompany seventeen young Gentlemen to Rome; who undertook that Journey rather out of Curiosity than Devotion, to see the Pomp and Magnificence of the Ceremonies that are then observ'd in that City. And the Jesuits persuaded me to go, hoping that by the sight of these Ceremonies I should be induc'd to embrace their Religion. I was easily prevail'd upon to comply with their Desires, and so we travell'd together to Rome, the other Gentlemen in Pilgrims Habit, and I in Japan Cloaths, and arriv'd there a little before the Death of the Pope, who being then sick, would not admit of any to come and see him; but we saw all the valuable Curiosities that are kept in that famous City. And the Jesuits at Avignon having given me Letters of Recommendation, I was nobly entertain'd there by the Jesuits of that City, who were very civil and obliging: But when they exhorted me to embrace the Christian Faith, I excus'd my self for not complying with their desire, and told them, That I intended to return again to Avignon, and to be baptiz'd there by the same Father who had brought me out of my own Country. After we had stay'd above a Month in Rome, we return'd again to Avignon, where I was civilly receiv'd by the Jesuits; who, as I have reason to believe, had charg'd the young Gentlemen my Fellow-Travellers to take care of me, that I should not make an escape; for they watch'd me as narrowly during the whole Journey, as Sergeants use to do a Prisoner.

Presently after my Return, the Jesuits ask'd me, how I lik'd all these Ceremonies I had seen at Rome? To whom I answer'd, That I was very well pleas'd with them, and did greatly admire them: But then withal I added, Since you condemn our Pagan Religion, because our Religious Worship consists only in Externals, how can you alledge your external Ceremonies in Confirmation of your Religion. To which they answered well enough, That they did not condemn our Ceremonies merely as external, but because they were destitute of any internal Virtue: Whereas the Christian Religion consists much more in its internal Power, than any external Shew: And therefore, said they, all our Ceremonies are unprofitable, unless the Heart be joyn'd with them; and we only make use of them to excite Men to Devotion, and to inspire them with greater Reverence and Fervor in the Worship of God. With this Answer I seem'd to be so far satisfy'd, that I made no Reply; tho' I might have told them, that we us'd the external Ceremonies of our Pagan Religion for the same ends and purposes as they do theirs. This indeed was a great scandal to me, to see the corrupt Lives of all sons of People, both great and small, at Rome, where they appear'd so publickly to be guilty of Adultery and Sodomy, that all Travellers might perceive them; which made me say to my self, Certainly if these Men did heartily believe their Religion, they would better observe its Preceps, and live according to it; but by their wicked Practices it appears, that they impose such things upon the common People, which they themselves do not believe to be true: Besides, I had heard so many Stories of the Miracles wrought by the Relicks of St. Peter, and other Saints, and chiefly of those which are pretended to be done in the Chapel of Loretto, which I believe to be false, that from thence I concluded their Relations of the Miracles wrought by Christ, to be no less false: So that my Journey to Rome was so far from inducing me to embrace the Christian Religion, that it rather prejudic'd me strongly against it.

"A DESCRIPTION OF FORMOSA"

Part III

George's Travels
THE SPURIOUS ACCOUNT OF HIS JOURNEY

AN ACCOUNT OF THE TRAVELS OF Mr. *George Psalmanaazaar,* a Native of the *Isle Formosa,* thro' several parts of *Europe;* with the *Reasons* of his *Conversion* to the *Christian Religion.*

WHen *Xaverius* the great Apostle of the *Indies* first arrived, with the *Jesuits* his Companions, at *Cangoxima* in *Japan,* in the Year 1549; they were civilly entertain'd by the Inhabitants of that Place, and after this the *Jesuits* and other *Missionaries,* being encourag'd by the kind Reception they met with, flock'd in great Numbers to *Japan,* and there boldly profess'd and propagated the Christian Faith, with good success, for many years. But since the Emperour of *Japan,* about the year 1616, (for certain reasons hereafter mention'd) has forbidden any Christian to come into his Dominions under pain of Death, and hath appointed Searchers in every City to examine all Forreigners, whether they be Christians or no, by this test, of Trampling upon the Crucifix; the *Jesuits* and other Missionaries of the *Romish-Church,* are so far from venturing to appear there bare-fac'd, or making publick Profession of the Christian Religion, and endeavouring to make Proselites, to it, that they industriously mask themselves under several disguises, lest they should be known to be Christians or Forreigners. And to this end they first Travel to *Goa, where there are Academies in which all the Oriental Languages are Taught;* and after they have Perfectly Learn'd the *Japanese* Language, and can speak it as easily and readily as any Native, Then they Cloth themselves in a *Japan* Habit, and so they venture to Travel into some Island within the Dominions of the Empire of *Japan.* When they are come there, they pretend to be Natives of some other Island in the same Empire, which is easily believ'd to be true by the Inhabitants, who have no suspicion of them, because they speak their Language exactly, and wear their Cloths after the mode of the Country. And thus having secur'd their admission into a City with safety, their next business is to prevent any umbrage of suspicion which may arise from their idle way of living, and to this purpose they seem as much concern'd for some Trade, or Employment, as if they really wanted means of Subsistance. Thus some set up for Merchants, Artificers, or Toy-sellers, others for School-masters or Pedagogues, to teach the Natives Children some Language they want to learn. And so every one acts his part, and Cloaks himself with some disguise, lest he should be discover'd to be a Forreigner, and consequently be oblig'd to trample upon the Crucifix. By this means they continue securely and free from danger, in any City of *Japan, for the space of four years*, which is the time allotted by their Superiors for their stay in those parts; after which time they are oblig'd to return to their own Country, and give place to other Missionaries who are then sent to succeed them.

Among the rest, there was a certain *Jesuit* of *Avignon*, whose true Name was Father *de Rode*, descended of an Honourable Family, who after he had learned the *Japanese Language* at the University of *Goa*, came into the Island of *Formosa*, about the Year 1694, which *was then and had been for some years Subject to the Empire of Japan*; and, being better qualified to be a Tutor to young Men than for any other Employment, he gave out, that he was a Native of *Japan*, descended of a rich Father, and that all his estate was divided among four Wives, and 13 Sons, he had left behind him, besides Daughters; that he being the youngest, the Portion which fell to his share was so small, that he was forc'd, at Twenty Years of Age, to leave his Fathers House, and Travel abroad, to get a Lively-hood by teaching the Latin Tongue. Which he had been taught; and that for this end he was come to *Formosa* after he had been in several other parts of *Japan*; by chance this Story happen'd to come to my Father's Ears, who sent for him, and after he had seen and discoursed him, he took him for a Learned and well-disposed Person; and therefore resolv'd to take him into his House to teach *me the Latin Tongue*. My Father acquainted me with the design, and told me that I should give over the *Learning of the Greek Tongue*, which I was then Studying because I might Learn it at any time in our own Academies, and that I must make use of the present opportunity of Learning the Latin Tongue by this Man, because he did not know when he should meet with the like opportunity. I readily submitted to my Father's Commands, as in Duty bound, and Father *de Rode* seem'd to be as glad of the opportunity as we were. My Father offer'd to allow him yearly 17 *Copans* for instructing me in the Latin Tongue, besides Diet and Cloths, which he accepted of; and so a Bargain was struck between them. Now a *Copan* is one pound weight in Gold, which in English Money, according to our way of value, is about six Crowns.

After this he came and liv'd at my Fathers House in *Xternetsa* the Capital City of *Formosa*, for the space of four Years, and behav'd himself so well in all respects towards my Father and my self, that we were both very well satisfi'd with him. He accompanied me to all places whither I went, except when I entred into our Temples, for then he always left me at the Gate, because, as he pretended, he being a *Japanner* was of a different Religion, from that which was establish'd in the *Isle* of *Formosa*, and therefore, he said, he would return home and worship his God after his own way. In the mean time he took care to instruct me *in all the Articles of our Religion, as exactly as* if he had believ'd it himself, and never spoke so much to me as one word of Christianity; and indeed he *employed his whole time* and pains in Teaching me the Latin Tongue, and instructing me in the Principles of our Faith, and of Moral Honesty: In fine, he appear'd to me, in all his discourse and actions, to be a Person of so great probity, honesty and candor, that I lov'd him almost as well as my Father. But at length, after four Years were expir'd, when I had acquir'd a competent knowledge in the Latin Tongue, he received Letters whereby he was oblig'd to return into his own Country; and therefore he begg'd the Favour of me, that I would acquaint my Father with his design of going away, and pray him, on his behalf, that he would dismiss him, and pay him the Salary that was due to him, according to the Agreement made between them; I lov'd him so well, that I was mightily troubled to hear of his departure, and therefore, being ignorant of the secret Mistery of his Mission, I did all that I could to divert him from leaving the place; but he declard that he was fully resolv'd to be gone, and Travel over the World, and see all other other Countries, and especially those that were Christian, which he extoll'd above all others, commending them highly upon several accounts, which *I afterwards found to be false*; In answer to this I told him, smiling, what are you mad to go among the Christians, where you will be kill'd for your Religion, as we kill them here upon the account of theirs: But he very seriously affirmed the contrary, and assured me that the Christians were very good Men, and that they were so far from any Cruelty, that they were always kind and generous to Strangers, and entertain'd them very Civilly and Nobly. Besides, he told me, that he did not believe those Men who were formerly in *Japan*, to be true Christians, as they pretended themselves to be, for, *said he, I have discours'd with many* Japanners *who* have been in Christian Countries, and they mightily commended both the Country and the Inhabitants; for the Country said they was the most Pleasant place in the World, and the Christian Natives gave them a very honourable reception, they showed them all the Curiosities of Art and Nature that were in those Parts, and when they came away, the Christians so loaded them with Gifts and Presents, that they returned home to their own Country with great Riches; upon which accounts the same *Japanners* continue still to Praise the Christians, and their Countries. My Tutor added farther, that in these Countries there is great plenty of those things which are here very scarce and precious, and besides there are many curious and valuable things in the Christian Countries, which were never seen nor known in *Japan* or *Formosa*. Lastly, he told me, that he would not stay any long time in Christendom, but only for the space of two or three Years at most, that he intended to spend three Years in his Travels, for as soon as he departed hence he would go to *China*, and from thence to the *East-Indies*, and after he had continued some time in these parts, he resolved to sail for *Africa*, and from thence into *Europe*, and there, continued he, I shall see *Spain, France, Germany, Italy, Holland* &c. The worst of which is more Beautiful and pleasant than this Island of *Formosa*. And at length after I have Travelled over all the parts of the known World, which are most Celebrated, either for the Curiosities of Nature, or the improvements of Arts and Sciences, I shall return home to my own Native Country, full Freighted with the Riches and experience I have gained, and then I shall have nothing else to do, but to spend the remaining part of my Life in Mirth and good Company, for all Persons of Ingenuity will be glad to see me, and delight to hear me discourse of the strange Rarities I have observed in other Countries, of their different and surprising Manners and Customs; of their Laws and Politicks in time of Peace and War, of the wonderful improvments of Arts beyond what is known in our Native Country, of their Methods of Trade and Commerce; And lastly, of the several Notable Accidents which happened to me in my Travels: And by these so Pleasant and useful Relations, I shall Purchase to myself great Honour and Esteem. These things he represented to me with such enticing Circumstances, that I could not but think with my self he had a mind to perswade me to go along with him, and I being then a young Man, about 19 Years of Age, was the more easily prevailed upon: For by the allurements he mentioned, he did so strike my Fancy, and excite my Curiosity of seeing the Christian Countries he so much commended, that I could not forbear to tell him, That if there was no Danger, but we might safely return again after five or six Years into our Native Country; I had a great mind to be his Companion, and Travel with him thro' all these Countries; But he, dissembling his design upon me, seem'd to be very averse to my Proposal, and told me in a feigned Passion, God forbid, that ever I should entice you away from your Father's House, If he should know that I had any such Design, what could I expect, but that he would presently put me to Death, and therefore I pray you, continued he, talk no more to me of any such things: But after he had inflamed my desire of seeing of the foresaid Countries, by the charming prospect he gave of them, this seeming refusal did rather irritate than extinguish my Curiosity, and therefore I was still the more importunate that I might accompany him in his Travels; and to remove his jealousies and fears, I promised him very seriously, that I would never speak one word of our design to any Soul alive, but carry it on with the greatest Secrecy that his own Heart could wish. But notwithstanding my promises he still seemed to continue backwards and unwilling to consent to my desire, upon account of the danger that attended him, which provoked me to repeat with greater earnestness my Solemn asseverations and vows of Secrecy and Fidelity; until at last after a long Conference, and reiterated supplications and assurances, he condescended to tell me plainly, that he had always a great opinion of my Candor and Sincerity, and he believed I had some respect for him, (as indeed I had a great Love and honour for him) that now he was resolved to show the great confidence he had in me, by putting his Life in my Hands, which he looked upon as the strongest obligation to Fidelity, and therefore continued he, since you are so urgent to be my Fellow-traveller, I am willing to take you along with me; but then you must be sure to be very cautious, and manage all things so secretly, that nothing may happen which will give the least Suspicion of our design. After the main matter was thus agreed between us, he used great Freedom with me, in concerting the manner of our Escape, and securing some part of a Fund for Subsisting us in our Travels. To this purpose, he told me one day, in our private Conversation, your Father is a rich Man and has great plenty of Gold both in Money and Goods, and since we are to undertake so long and expensive a Voyage, it will be very convenient that we should take a good quantity of this Gold along with us, which will help to defray our Expences; but then to prevent all Danger of Discovery, nothing of this nature must be attempted, till such time as we intend to make our escape; and then about midnight we shall seize upon all the Gold and Money we can safely come at, and pack up our Bagage, and march off to the *next Port, were we may have a Ship*.

Having thus fix'd our matters, when the time appointed came, I made ready to be gone, and carried off with me, (besides other Necessaries for our Journey) twenty five pound weight in Gold, partly in Money and partly in *Vtensils; viz.* one piece of coin'd Gold, call'd *Rockmo* weighing; 8 pounds 3 *Copans*, whereof each being a piece of coin'd Gold weighs 1 pound; and 14 pound weight of Gold in Utensils, as Pots, Plates, *&c.* besides what I took in Silver and Steel Money, to the value of 600 Crowns or thereabout. With this Stock of Gold and Money, my Tutor and I set forth, having left all my Father's Family fast asleep, and we arrived about midnight at a Port of the Sea, called by the *Formosans Khadzey*, which is distant from my Father's House, in *Xternetsa*, about Nine *English* Miles: And there I met with one of my Fathers *Baleons* or Gallies, and commanded the Steers-Man to carry me to *Luconia*, pretending I had earnest business to dispatch there for my Father. *Luconia* is the chief of the *Philippine* Isles, distant from *Khadzey* about 100 Leagues, where we stay'd about Eight Days, during which time, I kept the Steers Man and all the Marriners there, lest they should return back and acquaint my Father where I was: And after Eight Days we found a Ship going to *Goa*, in which we embark'd, and arriv'd at *Goa*, distant from *Luconia* about a 1000 Leagues. There we continued about six Weeks, during which time we were very Civily and Nobly treated in the Monastery of the Jesuits, which my Tutor told me, was a House built by the Christians for entertaining Forreigners, and indeed by the kind reception we met with there, he did in some measure convince me of the truth of what he had formerly told me in *Formosa*, about the Probity and

Generosity of the Christians. After six weeks were expir'd, we went a board on Ship that was going from *Goa* to *Spain*, and arriv'd at *Gibralter*, in the space of Nine or Ten Months, where I was forced to stay for the space of five Weeks, being very much indisposed by the change of Climates, Air and Diet. At length after my Recovery we sailed from *Gibralter* towards *Toulon*, which is a Sea-Port-Town in *France*, where I saw a great many several sorts of Monks in different Habits, which seem'd strange to me, whereupon I ask'd my Tutor who these Men were, who told me they were Men come from different parts of the World for Trade and Commerce; and that every one of them wore the Habit of his own Country. And as we passed through *Thoulon*, *Marseils* and *Aix*, in *Provence*, I observed a great many Crosses on the Road, which moved me to tell my Tutor; surely there must be a great many Thieves in this Country where there are so many Gallows; but he answer'd, that these Gallows were only intended to fright Thieves and Robbers, by the Terror of such a violent Death. And we arrived at last at *Avignon*, before I knew my Tutor to be a Christian: But after we went into the Monastery of the Jesuits there; when I perceived the Porter call him by his Name, show him great respect, and talk to him in their Langage, I began to doubt of my Tutor whether he were not a Christian; and when I saw all the Fathers of the Convent come to him, salute him, and congratulate his safe Return; and after that, all his Kindred, and lastly all the Noble Men and Gentlemen of the City, came to visit him, and express their great joy for his safe Arrival; I could no longer keep silence, but ask'd him, Whether he had not been here before? How it came to pass that so many People in this City received him very gladly, and pray'd him to tell the me truth how the matter stood. Whereupon he confess'd to me ingeniously, that he was a Native of that Country; and that he did profess the Christian Religion; and then he assured me, that I should find all things true, both as to the Country and the Inhabitants, which he had told me in the Isle of *Formosa*. I have indeed added he, brought you from your

Father's House; but you know you were very willing and desirous to come along with me: And now I will *make you a very fair offer*, If you be willing to Learn, we will Instruct you in all the Principles of our Religion; and if you can be perswaded to embrace it, we will take care to provide so well for you, that you shall live as well here as you did at home: But if you have a mind to return into your own Country, we will assist you and furnish you with Necessaries for your Journey. This last part of his Proposal was only a Copy of his Countenance, which he never intended to make good, as appeared by the sequel: For he knew, there was no advantage to be reap'd by my return into my own Country, which he might expect if I continu'd there, by making a Convert of me to their Religion. However, this Discourse made me very thoughtful and anxious, and when I reflected seriously upon my condition, and the great danger to which I was reduc'd, I was so astonish'd, that I knew not what to say or do: Yet I concluded with my self, it would be my safest and best way, to give my Tutor and the rest of the Fathers good Words, and carry my self fairly towards them, lest they should treat me after the same way as we do the Christians in our Country; of which I was sometimes very apprehensive. At length to show my self tractable, and gain their good Opinion, I made them this frank offer, That if they could show me greater Evidence for the truth of their Religion, than I could show for the truth of mine, I was ready to renounce my own Religion and embrace theirs. Father *de Rode* presently accepted of this Proposal, hoping I would yield to his Arguments upon the first onset: But to procure himself the greater Glory, he gave out that I was the Son of a King, *(how truly God knows)*, and that I had accompanied him into *Europe*, out of a desire I had to embrace the Christian Religion.

There were only three ways by which they could hope to make a Convert of me, by Arguments and Demonstrative Proofs, by flattering Insinuations and fair Promises, or by Threats and Violence. By Arguments they could not convince me, for I was able to show *greater absurdities* in their Religion than they could prove in mine; and particularly, in their Doctrine of Transubstantiation; Against which I argu'd several ways: As, First from the Testimony of our Senses, *viz.* of seeing, feeling, tasting, all which do assure us, that it is Bread, which we receive in the Sacrament and not Flesh: If therefore we believe our Senses, we cannot believe that the Substance of the Bread is chang'd into the natural Flesh of Christ, which is corporally present in this Sacrament: And then I prov'd that we must believe the Testimony of our Senses; because upon them depends the certainty of the Relations we have concerning the Miracles wrought by Jesus Christ, for the confirmation of his Doctrine: For if those who were Eye-witnesses, could not be certain by their Senses, that such Miracles were wrought, as are related in the Life of Christ, than we have no certainty of the truth of these Relations which depends upon the Testimony of those Eye-witnesses, who affirm that they saw such Miracles wrought by Christ, and consequently all the Evidence for the truth of Christianity, from the Miracles pretended to be wrought in confirmation of it, is subverted and destroyed. Thus the belief of Transubstantiation is inconsistent with the Belief of these Miracles; for if we believe them we must allow the Testimony of Sense to be a sufficient proof of them; But if we believe Transubstantiation we must renounce our Senses, and deny them to be a certain proof of any thing we see or feel.

Secondly, I argu'd, That their Doctrine of Transubstantiation must be false; because the same Body cannot, at the same time, be in two distant places: But according to their Doctrine, the same Body of Christ was corporally present in a 1000 distant places at the same time, *viz.* in all those places where this Sacrament is Celebrated, over the face of the whole Earth, however distant and remote from one another. Their distinction which they applied to this Argument, That the same Body could not be in more places than one *Circumscriptive*, but only *Definitive*, appear'd to me frivolous and impertinent; for still it appeared to me impossible, that the same Body should be Corporally present (tho' it were only *Definitive* as they called it) in several distant places at the same time; for then the same Body might be kill'd and dead in one place, while it was alive in another.

Thirdly, I argu'd, That when Christ said at the Institution of this Sacrament, *Do this in remembrance of me*, he supposed that he would be absent from them when they should Celebrate this Sacrament; for it is neither necessary nor usual to remember a Friend present, but only one that is absent; And therefore, these words of Christ, *Do this in remembrance of me*, do plainly imply, that he is not Bodily present (in this Sacrament.) I argu'd that their Doctrine of Transubstantiation could not be true, because it supposed, that the accidents of Bread (as they call them) remained without the Substance, and the Substance of Christ's Flesh was corporally present without the accidents that are peculiar to Flesh, both which appeared to me impossible: For I cannot conceive how the whiteness of Bread can subsist, when there is nothing that is white, and how there can be the Substance of Flesh, which can neither be seen, felt nor tasted.

These were some of the Arguments I urg'd against their Doctrine of Transubstantiation, to which I could never receive a Satisfactory Answer, and tho' they alledg'd several Arguments to turn me from Heathenism; yet because I thought there were greater absurdities in their Religion than they could shew in mine, I still adhered to my own Religion. And therefore finding that by Arguments they could not prevail, they attempted to bribe my Affections, and so win me over to their Party, by many fair Promises, and wheedling Insinuations; But I *knew so well their Insincerity and cheating Tricks*, by their counterfeiting themselves to be Heathens in *Formosa*, and by breaking their Promise of allowing me Liberty of Conscience, that I could put no Confidence in any Promises they made me. And besides, I very well knew, that I could have more Riches and Honour, if I should return into my own Native Country, than I could expect from them. In fine, the earnest desire and probable hope I had of returning to my Father, being join'd with the fear of continuing in this remote Country, far distant from my Relations, among Strangers and Hypocrites, made me flight all the offers they made me: Which induced them at last to use Threats and Violence; and these I endur'd with great meekness, and endeavour'd to mittigate their Anger with soft words, while in the mean time, I was contriving and preparing, by the most probable means I could think of to make my escape out of their Hands.

I continued at *Avignon* for the space of 15 Months, six in the Monastery of the Jesuits, and nine in other places: While I continued in the Monastery, I found they were continually teasing and persecuting me with Enticements, and Arguments to embrace their Religion, and therefore to get rid of them, I pretended a great desire to hear their publick Prelections, for which end I went sometimes to their Schools of Philosophy, and sometimes of Theology. But being still liable to their troublesome Solicitations, at last I left the Monastery, and took a private Lodging in the City, where I lived at my own proper Charges: And because they had a great part of my Money in their Hands, which they thought I would not leave behind me, they gave me leave to satisfie my Curiosity, and ramble over the Countries round about, which I did, travelling from City to City, for the space of six Months: After I returned to *Avignon* again, I continued there only for the space of three Months, from the time I first took a private Lodging in that City. And they welcom'd me, and seem'd at first to receive me very kindly, but when they found that I put off from Day to Day, to declare my self a Convert, then they begun to attack me more closely, and told me plainly, We have waited a long time to receive you into the Bosom of the Catholick Church, and used many arguments to convince you of the truth of our Religion, but since you still continue obstinate, we must desire you to take notice, that we can no longer bear with your delays; for hitherto we have entreated the Fathers Inquisitors that they would not give you any trouble, which they have forbore to do upon our request: But now since you have rejected all the fair means that we have used for so long a time for your Conversion, they are resolved not to wait any longer. And to show they were in good earnest, about eight Days after there came Letters from the Grand Inquisitor, expresly requiring that I should be put into the Inquisition, unless I would embrace the Christian Religion. Whether these Letters were real or supposititious I know not, but this is certain, that the Inquisitors show'd me such Letters, and withal told me, *That if I did not change my Religion within Ten Days, they were obliged to imprison me.* The Jesuits were present, when these things were done, who having consulted with the Inquisitors, they both agreed to allow me Fifteen Days wherein to make a publick profession of their Religion. The reason of granting me this further time, was this, because the Day on which they spoke to me was the first of *August*, and the 15th of that Month being, according to them, the Day of the Assumption of the Blessed Virgin, they had a great mind that I should publickly declare my Conversion, and be baptized on that Solemn Festival. All these Proposals I was forc'd to submit unto, and durst not refuse them in my present Circumstances: Whereupon they, conceiving good hopes of me, began anew to explain to me the Mysteries of their Religion, which they did by similitudes; Thus, for Example, they illustrated to me the Mystery of the Trinity, by the similitude of a piece of Cloth which is thrice folded, which, notwithstanding the three folds, is one and the same Cloth. They would never allow me to read the Bible, but they furnish'd me with abundance of Books about the Miracles pretended to be wrought by some of their Saints, in confirmation of their peculiar Opinions. For the first four or five Days, of the Fifteen which were allotted me, I heard, with great appearance of submission, all the demonstrations they pretended to give for their Doctrines, and when they answered my Arguments with Philosophical distinctions, and used a multitude of hard words, which were to me unintelligible, I granted all that they said, and confessed they had almost made me a Convert. For when I said that I could not understand those Answers, or Philosophical Arguments; This Father *De Rode* began to say to me, My dear, since you cannot understand what this Reverend Father says, I will explain it to you in your own *Japanois* Language; and so instead of explaining it to me, he said, *My dear Son, You see that the Fathers Inquisitors, have a great mind to put you into the Inquisition, because you won't confess your self a Convert; therefore it would be better for you to say that you understand what they say, than to be any longer obstinate; their Arguments are very well grounded and reasonable, but you cannot conceive the strength of them; therefore let me desire you to say publickly, that you are now perswaded of the goodness of their Arguments, and that you don't require any more.* So I was obliged to speak in Latin, and say, *Now I understand very well, Let us come to another Article.*

But still I trusted, under God, to my heels, hoping by some means or other to get out of their Hands, and to run away in such a Road that they should not be able to find me out again. After Ten Days of the Fifteen were expired, I had sold all that I had, and then I attempted to get out of the City, but I found that the Centinel, who watched at the Gate to which I came, was expresly forbidden to suffer me to go out; such care was taken by the Inquisitors to prevent my Escape. However I did not despair, but being returned to my Lodging, I put off my *Japan* Clothes, which I had hitherto wore, and clad my self after the Mode of the Country; and then I attempted to pass out by another Gate: But I was so much taken notice of by all the People that were in the City, that the Soldier who stood Centinel at that Gate, knew me under the disguise of my Clothes, and stopp'd me. This second disappointment frighted me not a little, but having recollected my Spirits, I considered that Money rules the World, and prevails over the generallity of Men, and therefore I offered the Soldier a Pistol if he would suffer me to go out, which he accepted of, and so let me go, hoping it could never be discovered that he was the Man that did it. Thus God delivered me out of the Hands of the Jesuits and Inquisitors, from whom I could expect no Mercy, if I had not in Hypocrisie professed their Religion, which I could never heartily believe.

Having thus made my escape out of *Avignon*, I travelled along the River *Rhone* with all the speed I could, as far as *Lyons*, from *Lyons* I went to *Salines*, from *Salines* to *Brisac*, and at last from *Brisac* I travelled by the side of the *Rhone*, as far as *Andernach*, where the Soldiers of the Elector of *Colen* seized me by force, according to the Orders they had received from the Elector, to Press all Passengers that came that way, to fill up the New Regiments he was Raising. There were then three Companies in *Andernach*, three in *Lintz*, and six in *Bonn*, whether all the other Companies resorted, being the place appointed for their Rendezvous; And when they were all come together, my Captain, thinking to gratifie the Colonel's Curiosity, acquainted him with what I had told him, that I was a Native of the Isle *Formosa*, belonging to Emperor of *Japan*, and by Religion a *Pagan*; that I had travelled from this far distant Country to satisfie my Curiosity of seeing *Europe*, having heard strange things about it: But the Colonel who was a *Savoyard*, and call'd *le Chevalier* St. *Maurice*, being a Bigot of the Romish Church, thought it a damnable thing to retain a Pagan in the Service of the Elector; who being informed about me, commanded me to be carried to some Jesuits, that they might endeavour to Convert me. Whereupon I was obliged to go with the Colonel and some other Officers to the Jesuits, with whom I was to dispute about Religion; tho' I knew very well by my former experience, that they are not able by strength of Argument to convince any Man, and much less, a *Jew*, a *Turk*, or a *Heathen*. And now, being well acquainted with their Opinions before hand, and the several Evasions and Distinctions they made use of to defend them, I was the better prepared to enter the Lists with the Jesuits, against whom I endeavoured to demonstrate; that there were greater Absurdities in their Religion, than they could show in mine; which I did with so much readiness and briskness, and such a fair appearance of Reason, that the Colonel cried out, like one astonished, It was not I that spoke, but some Devil that spoke within me. At last one of the Jesuits took me aside to a private place, and told me, that I was in a most miserable condition, if I should continue in the *Pagan* Religion, but if I would declare my self a Convert to the *Romish* Faith, he was able to obtain great things for me from the Prince Elector; But I told him he should first convince me of the Truth of his Religion, before he made me any such Promises; which he not being able to do I slighted his offer, and continued still in my own Religion. Whereupon the Colonel was so exasperated against me, that he threatned to throw me into Prison, and feed me with Bread and Water, until such time as I should declare my self a Convert. But my Captain, who was much the honester Man of the two, having seized me by force, would not suffer any hurt to be done me; and therefore prayed the Colonel to permit me to go off, and to grant me a Pass, for traveling whethersoever I would; which was presently done. After I got out of *Bonn*, I continued my Journey till I came to *Colen*, and there the Centinel who kept the Gate seized me again, and carried me before the Captain of the main Guard, to whom I showed my dismission out of *Bonn*, upon the account of my Religion; but he told me, *If others be Fools, I am not, though you are a* Pagan, *you may serve in the Army as well as the best* Christian, and so I was obliged to List my self a Soldier in that Regiment. The Colonel whose Name was *Buchwald*, and the Major who was my Captain, and whose Name was *Warmsdorff*, were both *Lutherans:* The Lieutenant Colonel, whose Name was *Vanduil*, was a *Roman Catholick*, and many of the Officers in the Regiment were *Calvinists*, and all of them belonged to the Prince of *Mechlenburg*, but the Regiment was hir'd by the *Dutch* for some Years.

The Colonel and my Captain sent for some *Lutheran* Ministers, whereof one was at *Colen*, another at a Village about an Hour distant, and two more who served in the *Brandenburg* Regiments. All these four came and disputed with me about Religion for a whole Day; but their Consubstantiation offended me as much as the *Roman* Transubstantiation.

For it is liable to many of the same absurdities with the *Romish* Doctrine, about the Eucharist; First, because it denies the certainty of our Senses in the proper objects, and consequently destroys their great Evidence of the Christian Religion, from the Miracles wrought in confirmation of it, which depends upon the Testimony of their Senses, who were Eye-witnesses of them. Secondly, The *Lutheran* Doctrine, as well as the *Romish*, supposes, that the Body of Christ which is now Glorious and Immortal in Heaven, is Corporally present in the Eucharist, and at the same time in all those places where this Sacrament is celebrated, which appeared to me impossible.

But besides these Absurdities, which are common to them both, the *Lutheran* Doctrine is encumbred with several that are peculiar to it: For first they say, that these Words, *This is my Body*, are to be understood literally, and that the Substance of the Bread is really present; so that according to their Interpretation the meaning of the Words is, This Substance of the Bread is really the Flesh of Christ, which is a contradiction *in terminis*; for it is plainly impossible, that the same Substance should, at the same time, be both Bread and Flesh. Secondly, They affirm that the Bread in the Eucharist is the Sacrament and Sign of Christ's Body, and at the same time that it is the real Body; whereas it is impossible that the same thing should be both the Sign and the Thing signified, or that any thing should be a sign of it self. Thirdly, They maintain that the Body of Christ is alive in the Eucharist (for they deny the Popish Sacrifice of the Mass, wherein the Body is slain and offered up) which being united to the Divinity, is certainly the object of Adoration, and yet they deny that it is to be worshipped. These and several other Arguments I urged against the *Lutherans*, whereby they perceived that they were not likely to convince me of the Truth of their Doctrine about the Eucharist: Whereupon the Minister who lived at the Village near *Colen*, took me home with him, and kept me there for Fifteen Days, and thither the Captain came also, and both of them joined together in making me many large Promises to entice me to declare for their Religion; but I continued inflexible, and could not be prevailed upon by any such Motives. After this the Lieutenant Colonel, who was a *Roman* Catholick, carried me to the Capuchins, and from them to the Jesuits; but all the means they could use with me proved ineffectual. At last the Officers that were *Calvinists* carried me to a Minister of their Church, who dealt so effectually with me, that he almost convinc'd me of the truth of the Christian Religion, because he removed those stumbling blocks which were laid in the way by the Papists and *Lutherans*: But when he proposed to me the Doctrine of *Absolute Predestination*, and endeavoured to prove it from Scripture, I was so shock'd by the apparent absurdity of it, that I begun to doubt of all those things he had convinced me of before: Whereupon I told him, if absolute Predestination was necessary to be believed, then it was a sign of my Reprobation, that I could not be perswaded to believe it. Besides I added further, That, supposing absolute Predestination I should never be condemned for my Infidelity, but because I was reprobated by an Absolute and Eternal Decree of God. And Lastly, I insisted upon this Argument, That I could not be perswaded to believe in Christ, unless I were certain that Christ died for me; but, supposing absolute Predestination, I could never be certain of this, because Christ died only for those who were to be saved by an absolute Decree, and it was impossible for me to know whether I was one of that number or no. These, and such-like arguments, I proposed to him, but he, to excuse himself for not answering them, pretended that I was obstinate and would not be convinced by Reason: And thus, after all the attempts that had been made to convert me to Christianity, I continued still firm in my old Religion. In the mean time our Regiment marched from *Colen* to *Boisleduc* in *Holland*, where some *Calvinist* Ministers came to see me, rather out of curiosity, than any design of converting me, whom I opposed with the argument against Predestination which I last mentioned, but could never meet with any satisfactory Answer to it. From the *Bosch* we marched to *Sluse* in *Flanders*, where we stay'd for the space of Three Months and a half, during which time, the most generous and candid Brigadier *Lauder*, who was then Governor of *Sluse*, invited to his House a Minister of the *French* Church, called *D' Amalvy*. This *French* Minister who had a good Opinion of himself, for a very learned Man, challenged me to Dispute with him about Religion, and time and place were agreed upon. When the Day came, there appeared a great multitude of learned Men, who came to hear us: And in the presence of them all *D'Amalvy* made me this offer; That if I could show greater Evidence for my Religion than he could show for his, he was ready to renounce his own Religion and embrace mine; and in return for this frank offer, I promised him to do the same thing, if he could give me clearer demonstrations for the truth of his Religion, than I could for mine. Having thus settled the Preliminaries, I was first to give an account of the God we adored, and our manner of worshipping him, which I did as well as I could *Extempore*; But when I told him, that we are commanded by our God to offer up Infants in Sacrifice to him, he stopp'd me, and ask'd, Does not this savour of Cruelty in your God, that he will have Men Sacrific'd to him; To which I answer'd, that it was indeed most cruel to require such Human Sacrifices; but from hence I took occasion to retort the argument upon him, by shewing that his God was yet more cruel, according to his Opinion of him, For if it be cruel to deprive Men of this Temporal Life, tho' by this means they are admitted to Eternal Life; certainly it is infinitely more cruel to create Men on purpose to make them Eternally miserable, and to condemn them to this Misery before they are Born, without any respect to the Good or Evil they shall do, and so to Sacrifice them to the Devil. To this Retortion he could not answer, and so I proceeded further to inform him, that our God did appear to us in the shape of an Elephant, an Oxe, &c. and that under these shapes we worshipp'd him: Against this Apparition of God under such Figures, he objected, That it was impossible that God who was Omnipotent, Infinite, Immense, Incomprehensible and Eternal, could be included in the Body of such a Beast. To which I answer'd, That if it is impossible for God to be included in the Body of such a Beast, he was bound to maintain the like absurdity by the Principles of his own Religion; For, said I, you believe that the Holy Ghost, who is God Infinite, Immense, &c. did appear under the shape of a Dove, which is much less than either an Elephant or an Oxe. To this he made no reply, and tho' there were many present who would have answer'd this and other Arguments, yet he commanded them all to be silent, and would suffer no body to speak but himself. In fine he exhorted me very much to the practice of Christian Humility and Meekness, as if he intended to reserve to himself alone the *Priviledge of Pride and Arrogance*, which I could plainly discern, by his Words and Actions, to be very predominant in his Temper. Thus this Conference ended, without producing any good effect upon me, and if by God's Providence I had not met with a better Guide to direct me in the Course I should Steer to arrive at a safe Harbour in this dangerous Sea of Controversies, I must have split upon the Rocks and Shelves of the absurd Opinions I met with among some sort of Christians, and adhear'd more obstinately than ever to the Idoltry in which I was educated. For I could never bring my Mind to believe such a Scheme of the Christian Religion, as was proposed, but not *demonstrated by him*; Such a System of Religion could never find entertainment with me, which places *Cerberus* in the very Threshold, I mean, which imposes as a necessary Article of

Faith, the horrible decree of absolute Reprobation, for this Doctrine gives a very odious and frightful Idea of a most Good and Gracious God, by representing him as Cruel and Tyranical to his poor Creatures, as one that designs and delights in their Eternal Ruine; it perfectly overturns all Religion, by destroying the use of all Laws, and their Rewards and Punishments, to those that are f etter'd with the Adamantine Chains of this fatal Decree; who according to the *Calvinists* are the greatest part of Mankind. But while I was in this uncertain and dangerous Condition, it pleased God, who is infinitely Wise and Good, and will not suffer that Religion which he has planted and maintain'd by his own Almighty Power, to be check'd in its progress by the Ignorance or Mistake of his Ministers: I say, it pleased this good God to provide for me such a Judicious and Honest Guide, as was very successful in all things relating to my Conversion, who proposed to me the Christian Religion in its Purity, without those Monstrous Doctrines of Transubstantiation, Consubstantiation and absolute Predestination: A Religion that was not embarass'd with any of those absurdities which are maintain'd by the many various Sects in *Christendom:* Whereof he gave me a Scheme in a Mathematical method by way of *Difinitions, Axioms, Postulata* and *Propositions*; which he divided into 2 Parts, whereof the first contains the grounds of the Christian Religion in general, the second contains the particular grounds of the Church of *England*, as it is a Society distinct from all Schismatical Assemblies. And first, the grounds of the Christian Religion he propos'd in the following Order, whereby I was, thro' God's Mercy, deliver'd from the Errors and Superstitions of my *Pagan* Religion.

THE ACCOUNT OF THE TRAVELS

PART IV

THE
SECOND
PREFACE

THE SECOND PREFACE

THE FIRST EDITION of this Book was quickly sold off, and there being a demand for more, the Booksellers consulted me about reprinting it, desiring I would recollect my self, add what I thought fit, and answer those Objections which the unmerciful Criticks have rais'd .against me and the Book. No wonder the Booksellers endeavour to remove all things that may hinder the sale of the Book; but for my own part, I am so secure in my Integrity, that the little Cavils of these disingenuous and inhospitable Men do not move me; however, the importunities of others have prevail'd, and I shall proceed to satisfie those scrupulous Gentlemen.

It does not seem strange to me that Men Should suspect the first Accounts of any remote places; for I do not imagine upon my return to Formosa, that even my own Countrymen will readily believe my Description of *England* and other parts of Europe. But, had not experience convinced me, I could never have thought that the censorious People here would have err'd so absurdly, as to take me rather for one of their Neighbours than for what I really am, a Japanese, born in Formosa, an Island many thousand Leagues distant from this of Great Britain. Suppose an Englishman was in Amsterdam and the Dutch there should say he was an Indian, how ridiculous would that assertion seem to him? He would answer only with scorn and contempt: Just so it is with me, who did not stir out of my Native Country Formosa, till I was nineteen Years of Age; and surely I cannot but smile at those People who would persuade me that I was born in Europe.

THE SECOND PREFACE

These unreasonable Scepticks tell you, there are Stories in my Book which they cannot believe, and therefore conclude me to be an Impostor; but methinks any consequence is more natural than this; for supposing that I have (tho' I assure you, I have not) ventur'd too far upon my memory, and written some Romantick Tales, yet these wild conclusion-makers may as well say that some of your English Writers were born in Japan, as deny me my Birthright, for there are more mistakes and blunders to be found in your own Historians than can ever be met with in my Description, &c, of my Native Country Formosa.

But here I beg leave to give a very short account of this Second Edition, and then I Shall go on to Answer the Objections, tho' not methodically, according to the thread of the Discourse, but as they have occasionally come to my knowledge. The first Edition of this Book was, I confess, imperfect, and wanted many curious and valuable Things, which long thinking, and the variety of questions since ask'd me, have at last brought fresh into my memory; the Booksellers found it impracticable to print these new matters by way of Appendix, and so there was a necessity to insert them in their proper places in this Second Edition. Many improprieties, vain repetitions, and indeed mistakes of one of the Translators of the former Edition, are left out, or corrrected in this; and I must acknowledge that the Gentleman who revis'd this, has mended the Language, not err'd a tittle from the Original, but to my great satisfaction has fully express'd my meaning, so that I can now say with *Pilate, What I have written, I have written.*

But the Reader I believe will agree with me, That it is more proper to answer the Objections here, and refer to the page of the Book to which they belong, than to put them in the body of the Book, and so be guilty of too long digressions. I shall pass over many little Arguments of my trifling Opponents, well knowing that Men of common Candour will reject them wheresoever they meet them, and therefore I shall only reply to Objections of the first Magnitude, and in which my Enemies seem to rejoyce and triumph; and how well I have perform'd this, let the World judge.

1 Object. Psalmanazar says that he was but nineteen Years of Age when he left Formosa, and that he has been about six Years in Europe. Is it not strange that He should so early be acquainted with the Customs and Manners of his Country? Or that he should give us so handsom a Description of it, after so long an absence.

1 Answer, This Objection proceeds from an Opinion that we Indians are Men of very poor intellects; for you would (on the other hand) wonder here if a young Gentleman, who has been most generously educated, could not give a better account of England than I have done of Formosa, tho' I assure you I had the best Education my Country afforded; but I find you think every thing that has the least appearance of ingenuity to transcend the capacity of an Indian.

2 Answ. If you imagine it to be impossible that I should be so well acquainted with my Country at those Years, or if I had, that I could not so long carry a Scheme of it in my Head, you do me more Honour than you are aware of, for then you must think that I forg'd the whole Story out of my own Brain, and if so, I am sure you extravagantly magnifie the fertility of my Invention, and the strength of my Memory; for he must be a Man of prodigious parts, who can invent the Description of a Country, contrive a Religion, frame Laws and Customs, make a Language, and Letters, &c, and these different from all other parts of the World, he must have also more than a humane Memory that is always ready to vindicate to many feign'd particulars, and that without ever so much as once contradicting himself. This (Reader) is my case. And hence the vanity of that English Gentleman, who would needs persuade me I was his Countryman, is very plain, for since he took it for a Forgery, he must conclude that no body had Wit or Judgment enough for such a contrivance but a true born Englishman.

3 Answ. But 3dly, I don't see the reason why a young Gentleman, who has all the advantages of Education, should not be able at nineteen Years of Age to give a tolerable Description of his Country. First, I am sure the Climate, Dimension, Product, &c, of Formosa may easily be known, 2ndly, As to our Religion, I confess my account of it to be imperfect, for I was not bred amongst Ecclesiastical Polititians. 3dly, As to our Government and Laws, I had all the reason in the World to be well acquainted with them, for I was born under such circumstances as obliged me thorowly to understand the Fundamentals of our Constitution. 4thly, As to the Habits, Cities, Palaces, Houses, &c. a Man of an indifferent memory, who has but once seen them, may easily retain an Idea of them. 5thly, As the Son of such a Father, I was engag'd to observe the Manners and Customs of the People. So that all Persons of my Condition must be very stupid if they cannot say as much of their own Countries as I have done of mine.

4 Answ. Lastly, I acknowledge that I have a treacherous memory, and should have forgotten many things, had I not been daily question'd about them, but now these frequent interrogatories have so deeply imprinted them in my mind that they can never be blotted out. *Vid.* first Preface.

2 Object. He tells us that he was learning *Greek* when his Father took de Rode into his House, and that the Greek Books were then thrown aside, because he could at any time learn that Language of their own Priests; but we are at a loss to know how the Japanese or Formosans came to be such Masters of Greek? *Vid. p. 175.*

1 Answ. This Objection is in a great measure answered already, Vid. p. 142.

However give me leave to add, that you may as well ask me how Formosa came first to be inhabited, and, because I cannot tell you, conclude there is not a Man upon the Island. Yet (that I may Say something on this Head) it is probable the Romish Missionaries first brought Greek amongst us, because we do not in our ancient

Writings find any Character of it, but the Books of our modern Priests and Philosophers are garnish'd with Greek Sentences and Quotations.

2 Answ. In Holland, and other places, I met with this Objection, and therefore would not have mention'd it in England, were it not an undoubted truth; but if any one will obstinately deny it, the best advice I can give him is, to go to Formosa, and, if he can, confute me.

3 Object. How could he get out of Formosa? And how came the Mariners to venture to carry him to Luconia, since he says (p.180) that the Emperor has forbidden any of his Subjects to leave his Dominions, without License under his Seal?

1 Answ. I heartily wish this Objection had never been made, because it will force me in some measure to discover my Father's Quality, which I have hitherto industriously conceal'd: Yet I must tell these quarelsome People, that this Law doth not reach Kings, Vice-Roys, Princes, Governours, Generals, or other wealthy Men, whole Estates and riches are sufficient caution against their leaving their Native Country, and my Father being under one of these Predicaments, and I his lawful Heir, I had no great reason to doubt a free passage to the Philippine Isands, for I had more cause to be afraid of my Father's displeasure than the Emperor's.

2 Answ. When such a young fellow as I gets a freak in his Head, he seldom considers the consequence: Besides, should the Emperor take offence at my rambling, I question not but my Father is able and willing to attain my pardon.

3 Answ. The Mariners knew me, and when I told him that I had business of the greatest consequence to do for my Father, they were well assur'd their Heads must have paid for't, had their refusal prejudic'd his Affairs.

4 Answ. Servants with us are rather commended than punish'd for obeying their

Masters, tho' in Crimes against the State; and therefore the

Steersman and Mariners ran very little or no hazard by carrying me to Luconia.

4 Object. Were there Mariners ever so far at Sea before? If not, it's probable they did not understand Navigation well enough to carry him a hundred Leagues, p. 181.

1 Answ. Our Mariners I confess are not well skil'd in Navigation, and it's probable my Father s Servants had never before been at the Philippine Islands; yet they are never without Chinese Maps, which tho' not So useful as what I have seen in Europe, are sufficient to direst us to our neighbouring Coasts.

2 Answ. As from Formosa to Japan, so from Formosa to Luconia abundance of little islands lie in a dircct line, and that Pilot must be mad, who in fair Weather mistakes so streight a Course; besides, they may guide themselves by other Observations that I am ignorant of.

5 Object. Luconia belongs to the King of Spain; and will the Spanish Papists there suffer a Pagan Vessel from Formosa or Japan to enter their Harbours?

1 Answ. Father de Rode had no reason to be affraid, because he knew he was going amongst his Friends; and truly he had given me such an honourable Character of the Crossmen (*vid. p. 177*) that I apprehended no danger; and farther, I believe he had inform'd them some way or other of his coming; for he has said be kept correspondence with most of the Papists in the East.

6 Object. What can be the meaning of his sailing from Goa to Gibralter? The first belongs to the King of' Portugal, and the other to the King of Spain; and there is no Commerce between these two places? *Vid. p. 182.*

1 Answ. Altho' these places are subject to different Princes, yet I think it does not follow that Ships from Goa may not touch at Gibralter, especially in times of Peace.

2 Answ. Father Fountenay, who understands these things as well as any Traveller, in the third Conference I had with him (just mention'd in the first Preface) ask'd me which way I came into Europe? I answer'd from Goa to Gibralter; some Gentlemen then present, reply'd, that there never was any Communication between these two places; but that Jesuit assur'd them it was matter of fact; which I wonder'd at, for I expected he would rather assert a falfsity, than confirm any thing I had said.

3 Answ. You mistake if you think the Ship deliver'd her Cargo at Gibralter, for She was bound to another Port (*Vid. p. 182.*) whose name I never knew, or have forgotten: But I am apt to believe she design'd for Lisbon; and the Jesuits of Goa, by their great credit had prevail'd upon the Captain to put de Rhode and I on shore at Gibralter, from whence we might have an safe passage to Thoulon and so to Avignon.

7 Object. Can it be thought that he Should make so long a Voyage, and not know the Captain's name, nor whether the Ship was Spanish or Portugueze?

1 Answ. I never expected to be called to an account for such trifles, otherwise I would have noted down every thing I had seen and heard, for nothing less I find will satisfie these carping Criticks. Could I imagine the Europeans would deny my Birth?

Or could I think them so absur'd as to take me for one of their Countrymen rather than a Formosan? I never look'd for such rude and disingenuous treatment from a People my Tutor had to much commended, and therefore I never enquire! after such little matters as what the Ship was, or the Cornmander's name.

2 Answ. I then thought that Europe had been but one large Empire like China or Japan, and that Spain, Freance, England &c. were Provinces subject to one Emperor. Besides, I did not dream that Ships were distinguish'd by proper names; and farther, I understood not a word the Captain and his Crew spoke, so that my Conversation was only with my Tutor who kept me in ignorance; lastly, during the whole Voyage I was indispos'd, and did not concern my self for any thing, but entirely rely'd upon my Tutor, who provided all Necessaries for me. And now let any impartial Man consider all these circumstances, and suppose Himself in my place, and then let him tell me whether thsee Objectors are not Egyptian Task-makers?

8 Object. He was about six Weeks in Goa (p. 181.) and five in Gibralter (p. 182.) and yet when he came to Thoulon (p.182, 183.) he admired the odd Habits of the Monks; this is unaccountable, for both the former places are ftock'd with Monks of all sorts.

1 Answ. This may be true, and yet it may be easily suppos'd that I did not see any of them; for I was too much indispos'd (p. 182.) at Gibralter to walk about and make Observations; and at Goa the Jesuits so nobly entertain'd me (p. 181.) in their Monastery, that I very seldom went abroad; how then can it be conceiv'd that in either of these places I should see and distinguish the great variety of Ecclesiastical Persons? I now find there are so many different Orders of Monk in the Popish Church, that during my five Weeks stay, even at Rome it self (p.190.) I did not see one third of them. At Goa I remember I Saw Jesuits, Dominicans, and (I think) Franciscans, but I am confident till I came to Thoulon I never met with Capouchins and reform'd Augustins; and it was the Habit of these two Orders that I so much wonder'd at.

9 Object, How came this young Pagan by such valid Arguments against Transubstantiation, Consubstantiation, and absolute Predestination? Is it not reasonable to think that he copy'd them from some of our best Casuists and polemical Divines?

1 Answ. This Objection, like the first, proceeds from the too mean opinion you have of the Intellects of us Indians, for certainly the first framers of all Arguments had little other helps than the strength of their own discerning Understandings; therefore if you will but allow the natural Faculties of Indians and Europeans to be equal, you must allow them equally able to draw natural conclusions.

2 Answ. The Arguments I brought against Consubstantiation and absolute Predestination I learned from the contending Parties, as you may see p. 201, 205. All that I have said against Transubstantiation, my reason suggested to me, one Argument only excepted, which by occasional discourse I afterwards met with, and because of its force was unwilling to omit it. The Translator finding the substance of the Arguments the same with the Great Tillotson and Others, may, for ought I know, make use of their words to save himself some trouble: But anyone who doubts, shall have the satisfaction of seeing my Latin Original.

10 Object. He tells us (p. 193.) That the Jesuits of Avignon shew'd him Letters from the Inquisitors, expressly ordering him to be put in the Inquisition, unless he embrac'd the Christian Religion in ten or fifteen days. We never heard till now that the Inquisition concern'd it self about Pagans; besides, he was a stranger, and did not desire to stay at Avignon, therefore all the power the Inquisition had over him, was only to expel him that Country, who it seems was already very willing to leave it.

Answ. I have said (p. 193.) that I knew not whether these Letters were forg'd or real. But the Pope who made the Inquisition, could easily have so interpreted the Laws of it, that I might have been a Sufferer; and I do not question had the Jesuits solicited the Pope in this case, but he would have given positive Orders to imprison aud punish me till I should declare my self their Convert. If these Letters were forg'd, then it's plain they did it to frighten me into a compliance; and this I believe was the truth of the matter, for there is no Man who is acquainted with the tricks of that wicked Society, but knows they will stoop to baser shifts to gain their ends.

11 Object. Why was he so fool-hardy as to own himself a Pagan at Andernach, who already had suffered so much for his Religion? p. 198.

Answ. I perceiv'd the People of Andernach to be generally Papists, but I very well knew the Inquisition had no power there, and therefore I thought I had nothing to fear. 2ndly, I was forc'd to serve as a Soldier, and at first had very little prospect of a discharge; I was no Occasional Conformist, I could not long conceal my Religion, and so I thought it best to acknowledge who and what I was. 3dy, When my Captain ask'd my name, that I might be enter'd in the Muster Roll, he took me for a Jew, but when I told him I was not, he reply'd, "You need not be afraid to tell your Religion, for be it what it will, you shall always have the free exercise of it; for here we tolerate all Religions, especially in times of War." This kind answer encouraged me to acquaint him with all my circumstances.

12 Object. Since he discovered himself so freely at Andernach, Bonn, Cologne &c. how comes it to pass that the Jesuits (who hold correspondence every where) did not take care to seize him and send him back to their Brethren at Avignon?

1 Answ. 'Tis probable the Jesuits may have an universal correspondence, and that Father de Rhode did write and search after me in all places where he had reason to think I was gone; but sure he did not dream of my being at Bonn or Cologne, for I found the Jesuits there had never heard of me.

2 Answ. But supposing they had been preacquainted with the whole Story, what could they do to me? I was now in another Country, and here they could not arrest me for Crimes committed at Avignon. 2dly, As I have said before, all Religions are here tolerated, 3dly. And consequently no Inquisition; and what reason then had I to fear the Jesuits, or any one whatsoever.

13 Object. Doth not his account of Formosa differ from all others? And doth not this render it false, or (to speak favourably) not much to be depended on? He Says (p. 2.) Formosa is 200 Leagues distant from Japan, others that it is 140, 150, or 160. He tells us 'tis about 60 Leagues distant from China, others assure us 'tis but 14, some say 20, some 30 or 33. From Luconia he says 'tis 100 Leagues, others are positive 'tis but 50, some 60, and others 80.

1 Answ. These People who contradict me differ among themselves, and methinks that, should render their Accounts at least as suspicious as mine.

2 Answ. I was not skill'd in Longitudes and Latitudes when I left Formosa, neither will I be positive that my Account of its distance from Japan &c. is exactly true: I may be something mistaken. For I never was out of Formosa till I came with de Rhode,

So what I have asserted is by hearsay, from my own Countrymen who have been Travellers.

2 Answ. The Europeans themselves are sometimes out in their Computations; no wonder then that my Countrymen, who are far the worst Geographers, are often mistaken.

3 Answ. Suppose I should ask ten Englishmen, how many Miles to France or Holland? Some would say more, some less, so no doubt but many of my Countrymen will say the distance is greater or less than I have asserted.

4 Answ. Let the Reader consider, that as the English Miles differ from the German, Italian, &c. So it's no wonder that our *Baikhs* or Leagues differ from yours. I take a Baikh to be about a Mile and a half English (more or less, as you say here). We reckon Formosa to be 400 *Baikhs* from Japan, which from the best computation I could make, is 600 English Miles: But if you reckon a *Baikh* to be but one of your Miles, then I find your Geographers and I agree pretty well. So that the difficulty lies in telling in English exactly how much a *Baikh* is, which I must confess is too hard for me to demonstrate.

14 Object. But his Historical Description of Formosa differs yet more from what all others have told us than his Geographical; Surely then that must be false that has so many witnesses against it.

1 Answ. Many candid Gentlemen have observed that this Objection rather confirms than discredits the Account I have given. For if any European has a mind to banter the World, and set up for a Formosan or a Chinese, his best way certainly is to read Candidius and others, and frame his Tale so that he may not be contradicted by the Romantick Authors that have already written of these Countries. Candidius (as I have told you in the first Preface) and others, say, That we have no Governour,

No Laws, &c. Why then should I assert we have, and contradict them almost in every thing they say? These Men assure you also that We are meer strangers to Letters; Why then should I be such a Fool to invent an Alphabet, and a Language, purposely to lessen my own Credit? Do but consider (tho' you are too Jealous and censorious) how easily you may be impos'd on; for had a Portugueze, a Spaniard, or any swarthy complexion'd Man (as you suppose a Formosan to be) who had read the Authors that treat of my Country, come into England before me, and had told his Story agreeable to what had before been falsy publish'd, you certainly would have believ'd him to be what he pretended, and yet you scruple to credit me, a Native of the place, and who have told you nothing but truth.

2 Answ. I have cited some of the many absurdities found in the Authors, and I appeal to any impartial Man, whether my reputation ought to stand or fall by their authority.

3 Answ. It is very material to remember how these Authors, as well as Father Fountenay, make no difference between Formosa, and Tyowan, tho' these Islands are about 12 Miles distant from each other, and indeed the latter is rather a knot of three little Islands. The Dutch, in the Account they give us of their Settlements in the Eastern Countries, tell us that they came to our Island Formosa much about the same time I have mentiori'd (*vid. p.4.*) and afterwards they say, "The Chinese came to Formosa, and suspecting that the Natives and the Dutch were conspiring against them, they banish'd the Dutch, out of that Island, from whence they went and Settled in Tyowan, where they built several Forts. Now I tell you (Chap.11.) That whilst the Dutch had Settlements amongst us, the Chinese came with a design to conquer our Island, this obliged us to call the

Dutch to assist us; but instead of that they prov'd false; however we fought with so much Courage against both, that at last we cut most of the Dutch to pieces, and clear'd the Island of the Chinese, the remaining Dutch were, banish'd. The whole difference consists in this. We charge the Dutch with ungrateful Treachery, and they excuse themselves as handsomly as they can. I must not omit taking notice how the Dutch contradict themselves, for whereas they say they settled in Tyowan after they were driven out of Formosa; yet in the last Collection of Travels (4 Vol. in Folio) they make these two Itlands one and the same.

As for example, We came (say they) from the Philippine Islands to Tyowan; and a little afterwards, From Formosa we returned. to the Philippines; and so in twenty other places you may there see the like confusion of names. This observation was made by a worthy Friend, who has read all Authors that make any mention of Formosa purposely to discourse me about it; but when he found the Dutch guilty of such a contradiction, he communicated it to me, that I might use it in my own defence.

4 Answ. Suppose these Geographers and Historians in the right, and that Tyowan and Formosa are only different Names for the same Island; yet then the worst that can be prov'd against me is, that I have mistaken the European name for my Country, and truly I must confess I cannot tell whether I have or no, for I am not sure I was born in that Isnd you call Formosa; that name was unknown to me till I came into Europe: We call it *Gad Avia*, the Chinese, *Pac Ando*, and you Insula Formosa, all which signifies the same: My quondam Tutor Father de Rhode assur'd me it was so, and he without question is well acquainted with these matters; in Avignon I remember more

People call'd me the Formosan than the Japannese; but if you will dispute this matter farther, I know not how to give you clearer satisfaction till I return to my native Country.

15 Object. How came it to be discover'd that Meryaandanoo

murther'd the Emperor Chazadjin since no body knew it but himself? p.8.

Answ. My business was only to tell you by what steps Meryaandanoo came to be Emperor, and how he by surprise made himself Master of our Island; I did not intend to write his Life; however, to satisfie these little Objectors, I shall inform them how he at last confess'd himself to be the Murtherer. In or about the 15th Year of his Reign, his Sons broke out into open Rebellion, and at last he was dethron'd and confin'd in the Dairo's Palace, where his troubles threw him into a dangerous Disease; then he earnestly desir'd to be visited by all the Kings, Vice-Roys, and Princes of the Empire, accordingly they all came from Yedo (where, as it happen'd, they were all at that time consulting about a new Election) to Meaco, and then he confessed himself to be the Murtherer; and that he had been too prophane, making a jest of all Religion, for which the Gods had justly Suffered him to fall under these Calamities, and now, says he, I am not, I acknowledge, worthy to live; so he drank a Coffee-dish full of Poison, and dy'd in the presence of them all.

16 Object. But this tragical Story of Meryaandanoo is so full of wonders, that it scarce can be credited.

Answ. This is such a silly Objection, that I should not have taken notice of it, had it not given me a fair opportunity of putting the People of this Kingdom in mind of a far more wonderful Trajedy; I mean their falsly accusing, condemning, and at Last contrary, directly contrary to their natural and sworn Allegiance, murthering King Charles the First before bis own Palace. So that if the tragical and wonderful Circumstances in the story of Meryaandanoo be Arguments against the truth of it, certainly after-Ages, and far distant Countries, will never believe the most unreasonable Murther of King Charles the First.

17 Object. Is it possible that any People should be so barbarously superstitious as to sacrifice so many thousand Children every Year?

p. 23, 31.

1 Answ. To incredulous ill-natural People this may seem impossible; but had I never heard of such a Custom till some honest Man bad assur'd me 'twas the yearly practice of this or that Nation, I protest I should not have much scrupled to believe it. For certainly where the People have not the blessing of reveal'd Religion, but are left to their own corrupted Wills and Ignorance, or, which is worse, are implicitly led by designing Pagan Priests, there is no Crime so black but these Wretches may be drawn in to commit, and nothing so inhumane but they may be persuaded to put in practice.

2 Answ. Histories Sacred and Prophane can furnish us with many Examples of this nature; but I shall content my self with what follows; The Prophet Jeremiah says, Chap. vii. v. 31. And they have built the high places of Tophet, &c. So burn their Sons and their Daughters in the Fire. &c. See also the Acts of the Apostles, Chap. vii. v. 43. Lactantius de falsa Religione, Sect. 21: Plutarch. Geft. Roman. 83 qaeft. Enseb. lib. 4. cab. 16. Levitic. Chap. 18. v. 21. And thou shalt not let any of' thy Seed pass through the fire to Moloch, &c. Since then this barbarous Custom was common in the most Learned and polite Nations, why should it seem incredible that my Countrymen, who are destitute of Revelation, and are the very Slaves of Priestcraft, should offer yearly so many thousand humane Sacrifices?

18 Object. If the Formosans had any such barbarous Custom, surely Candidius would have told us of it?

Answ. I think I have already in my first Preface and elsewhere said enough to detect the forgeries of Caudidius. But let us compare another cruel Custom which he falsly fathers upon my Country, with this of sacrificing Children, and I dare say his will be found more barbarous and improbable; and yet his Lyes are received as Truths, and my Truths rejected by some disingenuous People as Forgeries. "Whensoever (says Candidius) a Woman under the Age of 37 finds her self with Child, she must send for one of the Priestesses

(Men he says have no share in divine Offices) who lays the breeding Woman upon the skins of wild Beasts, and then jumps and dances upon her Belly till she miscarrieth. In the Year 1628, (he says) one of my Countrywomen told him that she had been to serv'd sixteen times, but that she was then big of her 17th Child, and she hoped she would go out her time, for she was now in the 38th Year of her Age. Now I appeal to all Mankind, if this be not a more barbarous Custom than what I affirm of the humane Sacrifices, and certainly more prejudicial to a Commonwealth. For Candidius himself says that many Mothers dye by this wicked practice; which in a few Years is enough to depopulate a very large Nation, especially considering that in hot Countries Women begin very soon to bear Children, but rarely are pregnant in their declining Age, so that if this Custom prevails, my Country must by this time be very thinly inhabited, for I dare fay few Formosan Women have Children after they are 38 Years of Age, eepecially if these murthering Priestesses have danc'd upon them fifteen or sixteen of their mortal Dances. Besides, this destroys both Males and Females, so that Polygamy to repair the loss is impracticable. And yet, notwithstanding all these pernicious inconveniences in this story, the fabulous Candidius was an Author of Credit with most People, till my Book came out and confuted him. But is it not strange that this and many other of his nonsensical incoherences should be readily believed, and yet what I truly say of human Sacrifices be disputed?

19 Object. We can believe that human Victims have (tho' very rarely) been sometimes offer'd, but that 18000 Boys should be yearly sacrific'd is incredible, for this practice would in a short time depopulate the Island, p. 23, 27.

1 Anw. This I think sufficiently answered in the 27th, 28th, 29th and 30th Pages of this Edition. And 1 desire the Reader to observe, that I assert the Law commands us to sacrifice so many, but I do not tell you it is matter of fact that we do every Year Sacrifice the full number.

2 Answ. We allow Polygamy (p. 53.) and that supplies us with a numerous Issue.

Suppose then eighty Males and eighty Females born in one street, and grant that Sixty of the Males are sacrificed, there will yet be left twenty Males for eighty Females, and there is no doubt but these Women will have as many Children as any eighty Women in another Nation where Polygamy is not lawful.

3 Answ. Most of these Children are sacrific'd very young; few of which (if they escap'd the knife of the Sacrificator) would live to the Age of one and twenty.

4 Answ. Do but consider how many Men, all fit for Marriage, go out of this Kingdom every Year, some to the East or West-Indies, some to Portugal, Italy, Germany, Flanders &c. and then tell me if more of your Men are not yearly destroyed than we sacrifice Children. And sure then one would think that Formosa is not in so great danger of being depopulated as England, where it is now a common observation, that there are four times more Women than Men.

20 Object. If Polygamy rather populates a Country, why has Turky fewer People (in proportion) than any other Country?

Answ. 'Tis observ'd that in Turkey, as well as in other places, the number of Males and Females born is near equal; if therefore one Man in Turky has thirty Wives, there must be twenty nine Batchelors, and had these been all sacrific'd when they were young, 'tis plain that Empire would be no less populous in one Age. Besides, it is not so probable that this Man who hath thirty Wives should have thirty Children every Year, as that a Formosan who hath six or eight Wives should have six or eight Children.

21 Object. He says, in the Chap. *Of Religion*, p.37, They were commanded to divide the Year into Months, Weeks and Days. And again, p. 23,27. to sacrifice so many Boys, and this is written m their *Jarhabadiond*; and yet in the Chap. *Of Weights And Measures*, p. 98.

he tells us, that before the Dutch came amongst them they had no names nor figures for numbers; how then were all these numbers written in the Jarhabadiond?

1Answ. By the word figures I understand such as are us'd in Europe; we had ways of making such and such marks for numbers before the Dutch came, but I could not properly call them figures, no more than you call so call your Milk-womens Chalk-scores, and yet you find they keep a fair reckoning with you.

2 Asnw. As I have told you, that in conversation we declared to one another what number we meant by signs on our Fingers, So we had Characters also to signifie these motions of the hands. Our great numbers were cast up by the help of Stones, or a Sort of Counters, and points made upon Paper. Some of our Noblemen by conversing with the Chinese learn'd their Hieroglyphicks. And this was all our Arithmetick.

22 Object. The Author must strangely forget himself, or the Translator misinterpret him, for he says (vid. first Edition, Chap. *Of Arms and Weapons*) the Japanese make such Scimiters as will cut at one blow a large Tree in sunder.

Answ. This is a good natur'd Objection; but had the expression been so strong in the Original, all that can be said is, that it had been an Hyperhole, which I believe is allow'd in all Languages, but I assure you the Latin runs thus, *Gladios fachiunt qui borem mediocriter magnam uno iztu abscindere possunt.* And now how that Translator who is old Dog at Latin came to make this mistake, I know not.

23 Object. If Gold be so cheap as he says (Chap. *Of Money*, p. 129.) Why do not the Merchants bring larger quantities from thence?

Answ. I was not of the Emperor's Council, and therefore will not pretend to tell the reasons why he suffers not the Merchants to export more Gold; this I know that the Merchants themselves say, tho' they pay such great Tribute for it, yet 'tis worth the while to carry it to China, tho' even there it's cheaper than in Europe.

2 Answ. Some of our Palaces are cover'd with Gold, and therefore it must be plenty; for tho' nothing is more proud and vain than an Indian Prince, yet he would not cover his large House with such Metal, were it not much cheaper than in other parts.

3 Answ. It may easily be supposed that when I came into England I was ignorant of the value of your Coin, and so could not make you understand how very cheap Gold was with us; which some Gentlemen to whom I lent my Manuscript observed and put into my hands Varenius's *Description of Japan*, &c. where is a Chapter spent in comparing our Japannese Money with your European Coins; I then made use of this Author, and still believe he is right in his computations; if not, let him answer for them.

24 Object. According to the Description he gives us of the Ships, &c. of Formosa, 'tis impossible they should live one day at Sea, for they are not mathematically or regularly built, &c. p. 128.

1 Answ. Our Ships, &c. are not perhaps fit for the Ocean; but we safely take such Small Voyages to China, Japan, or the Philippine Islands; we Coast it indeed as much as we can; and if we perceive a Storm, we put into any Creek and drop Anchor.

2 Answ. I will not pretend to defend the regularity of their building. I know little more of the Mathematicks than one born blind doth of Colours; I have given you the figures of these Vessels as near as I can remember; and I leave the dissection of them to the Mathematicians.

25 Object. If he is resolved to continue a true Chriftian, Why doth he talk of returning home, where he must renounce his Religion or be crucified? p. 16, 159, 161.

1 Answ. I could say several things to this Objection, but at present it is not proper to publish them; however, I will in private satisfie any Member of the Church of England, who is not contented with what follows.

2 Answ. If a Man puts a question to me, I ought to take the question in the same sense he asks it, and so fairly, answer it; this being granted, I shall, before I reply, only put the Reader in mind how much our hatred is encreased against the Christians: Ever since the great Persecution, the People have lost all the good Principles the Jesuits preach'd, and retain only a hateful remembrance of their Tricks, Frauds and Designs to extirpate all the Pagans; these Notions the Priests industriously keep fresh in our memories; so that now we take a Christian to be one who worships a Crucifix and other Images, that makes and eats his God, that believes one Priest to be the supreme Head of his Church, and that he is strictly obliged, by his Religion, to persecute and destroy, &c. all those who will not submit to this Head of his Church.

Now let the Reader consider this, and tell me whether (I knowing by a Christian or Crossman they only mean a Man of such Principles just mention'd, which I from my Soul abhor) I fay, let the Reader tell me whether I am not oblig'd, at my return, to deny my self to be such, and even to trample upon the Crucifix as a confirmation that I had told them the truth? Vid. p.161, 162.

Thus I think I have answered all the Objections of moment; as for those of less weight, I chose rather to explain them in their proper places in the Book, than too much to swell this Preface. But whosoever is not entirely satisfy'd with what I have said, may come to me, or I will take it for a favour if he pleaseth to send me his scruples in a Letter, and I promise to give him a speedy and plain Answer: Any of the Booksellers, for whom this Book is printed, can direct you to me.

But I must not conclude before I have given a true Account of a Conference I had with the Excellent Captain Halley, Savilian Professor of the Mathematicks in the famous University of Oxford, for many People talk of it.

'Tis about a Year since I had the honour to meet Captain Halley with some other Gentlemen at a Tavern; they ask'd me the usual questions about my Country, and I returned satisfactory answers; at last, says the Captain, Doth not the Sun shine down the Chimneys in Formosa? I answer'd negatively; at which they were surprized, for most Geographers place our Island under the Tropic of Cancer; but I went on, telling them that granting Formosa was exactly under the Line, it was impossible the Sun should shine down the Chimnies, for they do not stand perpendicular, but the Smoak is carried through the Walls of the House by crooked pipes, and their ends are turn'd directly upwards, the better to convey it into the Air. Pray Sir (says the Captain) when you stand upright in the hottest weather how is your Shadow? I reply'd very short, insomuch that it can scarcely be discern'd. The last question was, How much twilight we have in Formosa? At first I did not understand his meaning, for I then knew very little English; but when he had explained himself, I reply'd that I never made any observations about it, for till I came into Europe, I never heard of a distinguish'd time from Day and Night. This is the whole of our Conference, tho' some People are pleas'd to invent a great deal more.

It is expected I should say something of the French Version of this Book, especially since that Translator pretends to have Latin Memoirs from me: I shall only tell you, that he imposeth upon the World; besides, 'tis very plain he compiled his from the first English Edition; tho' he has taken but little care to stick to his Original: It would not be altogether useless to take notice of the many gross Faults in the French Translation, but I have already trespassed too long upon the Reader's Patience, and therefore put an end to this Preface.

London, June 12.
1705

BIBLIOGRAPHY

Foley, Frederic J. *The Great Formosan Impostor*, Jesuit Historical Institute. 1968.

Lynch, Jack. "Orientalism as Performance Art: The Strange Case of George Psalamanazar," talk delivered at the CUNY Seminar on Eighteenth-Century Literature, January 29, 1999.

Swiderski, Richard M. *The False Formosan: George Psalmanazar and the Eighteenth-Century Experiment of Identity*. San Francisco: Mellen Research University Press, 1991.

Memoirs of ****, commonly known by the name of George Psalmanazar, 1764.

Boswell, *Life of Samuel Johnson*

Jonathan Swift, *A Modest Proposal*

R. Needham, "Psalmanazar, confidence-man", *Exemplars*, 1985.

Oxford Dictionary of National Biography, Oxford University Press, Sept 2004.

Acknowledgments

I would like to thank the Sinologist, writer and historian Frances Wood for suggesting this project. I had never heard of George Psalmanazar before she mentioned him. Also to *baijiu* afficionado Derek Sandhaus for his suggestions on improving the first part.